COOKING AT A GLANCE

CHICKEN

BLOOMSBURY

This edition published in 1995 by
BLOOMSBURY PUBLISHING PLC
2 Soho Square
London WIV SPE

Conceived and produced by
WELDON OWEN INC.
814 Montgomery Street
San Francisco, CA 94133
Telephone (415) 291-0100
Fax (415) 291-8841

A member of the Weldon Owen
Group of Companies
SYDNEY • LONDON • SAN FRANCISCO

ISBN: 0 7475 1987 0

A CIP record for this book is available
from the British Library

A WELDON OWEN PRODUCTION

Printed by Kyodo Printing Co.
(S'pore) Pte Ltd
Printed in Singapore

Cover Recipe:
Sherried Chicken with Orange Sauce,
page 64
Opposite Page:
Poussins with Cherry Sauce, page 31

2

WELDON OWEN INC.

PRESIDENT JOHN OWEN

PUBLISHER WENDELY HARVEY

MANAGING EDITOR TORI RITCHIE

CONTRIBUTING EDITOR JANE HORN

AUSTRALIA/UK EDITOR JANET BUNNY

DESIGNER PATTY HILL

ASSISTANT DESIGNER ANGELA WILLIAMS

PRODUCTION STEPHANIE SHERMAN, MICK
BAGNATO, JAMES OBATA, AND TARJI MICKELSON

FOOD PHOTOGRAPHER CHRIS SHORTEN

STEPS PHOTOGRAPHER KEVIN CANDLAND

FOOD STYLISTS SUSAN MASSEY AND
VICKI ROBERTS-RUSSELL

PROP STYLIST LAURA FERGUSON

ASSISTANT FOOD STYLIST DANIEL BECKER

CONTENTS

INTRODUCTION	6
THE BASICS	7
ROASTING & BAKING	15
GRILLING & BARBECUING	35
FRYING & SAUTÉING	49

STIR-FRYING 71

BRAISING 85

MICROWAVING & POACHING 105

GLOSSARY 118

INDEX 120

Introduction

A PERFECTLY ROASTED CHICKEN, crisp and golden, is more than just Sunday lunch. Simple and succulent, it represents home cooking at its best.

But roasting is only one way to make the most of the savoury taste of chicken. Because this bird is such a superb carrier of other flavours, a wealth of memorable dishes has been created by talented cooks the world over to show it off. *Coq au vin*, a herb-and-wine-simmered dish, is a glory of the French country table. Latin cultures relish fajitas, tortilla-wrapped strips of grilled or sautéed chicken and peppers, while in India, chicken is infused with an enticing depth of flavour from a coating of yogurt and curry spices.

Chicken is now more popular than ever. It is widely available, economical and, because it is relatively low in fat and a good source of protein, increasingly appreciated for its contribution to a healthy diet. If you are looking for new ways to prepare this old favourite, there are sixty new recipes in this volume especially for you. Behind every one is many years of kitchen experience and testing by culinary experts.

Chicken is also the ultimate guide for anyone in need of practical information. Every important technique — from cutting up a whole bird, to boning and skinning, to making stock, plus a thorough discussion of cooking methods — is demonstrated in vivid photographs and explained in easy-to-follow language. It's all there at a glance, as if you were looking over the shoulder of a professional chef.

An introductory chapter covers the basics of poultry handling and preparation, while succeeding chapters focus on a particular cooking method. Each builds on what you've already learned, with additional steps, special techniques, and tempting recipes. Every chapter is colour-coded, and every recipe features a "steps at a glance" box that uses these colours for quick reference to the photographic steps that illustrate its preparation. Valuable tips appear on virtually every page, from basic equipment needs to helpful hints from the experts and stylish serving ideas. A glossary provides an overview of the ingredients used in the book.

Whether you are a novice or an experienced cook, you will find new ideas to tempt you such as Spicy Spanish Kebabs, Honey-glazed Drumsticks, Butterflied Citrus Chicken, and Poussins with Cherry Sauce. The step-by-step sequences will explain the fine points in preparing such impressive fare as Roast Chicken with Pecan Rice Stuffing or Chicken Breasts with Tomato-Mint Pesto. To help you plan a menu, these and all the other recipes in the book are beautifully photographed along with suggested accompaniments. So don't hesitate to get started. You'll be amazed at how easy it is to master chicken cookery *at a glance*.

Spicy Spanish Kebabs,
page 47

The Basics

Steps in Cutting Up a Whole Chicken

BASIC TOOLS FOR CUTTING UP CHICKEN

To cut through cartilage and joints, you will need a sharp boning knife and poultry shears or kitchen scissors. Work on a surface that is dishwasher safe, such as an acrylic cutting board.

POULTRY SHEARS

ACRYLIC
CUTTING BOARD

BONING KNIFE

CHICKEN IS SO VERSATILE that almost every part is useful, as the delicious recipes in this book will demonstrate. Packaged, ready-to-cook chicken pieces are widely available and a great convenience, but cutting up a whole chicken yourself is not the daunting or time-consuming task some view it to be. In fact, it is easily learned, quickly accomplished, and is such a basic technique for working with poultry that it should be part of every cook's repertoire, even if used only occasionally. It provides a foundation for the entire book because once you are comfortable with handling a whole chicken, you are better able to put the parts to good use.

A further bonus: When you are the butcher you not only produce portions that are custom-trimmed to suit your needs, you also save money. A whole chicken is usually less expensive to buy than an equivalent weight of poultry pieces because there are no labour costs built into the price.

This section will take you step by step through cutting up a whole bird. Another name for this technique is *jointing,* because you cut through the elastic tendons and cartilage that surround the joint rather than through

solid bone. With practice, you will be able to locate this soft tissue by touch, and the process will be much faster.

Very little specialised equipment is required to cut up a chicken other than a sharp, good-quality boning knife, poultry shears or kitchen scissors, and a dishwasher-safe acrylic cutting board or wooden board. Avoid boards that are made of hard plastic; they will damage and dull your knives. Always wash your hands, your tools, and the cutting surface with hot soapy water after working with raw poultry to keep them free of bacteria.

Boning knives are typically 10 in/25 cm long, with thin, tapered, flexible blades that let you manoeuvre around the curves and indentations of meat and bone. Keep your boning knife (or any knife) sharp so it will slice cleanly without slipping. The safest knife is a sharp knife. Poultry shears use a spring-lever action for more cutting power, although a pair of sturdy kitchen scissors will work almost as well in most cases.

Don't put your tools away after the bird is jointed. On the following pages, you will also learn how to quickly and deftly bone breasts and legs, and how to remove the skin.

cutting through a joint or carti-lage does less damage to the knife than cutting through bone

to skin a leg or thigh, see pages 10 and 11

holding the wing away from the body lets you see where to cut

STEP 1 CUTTING OFF LEGS

Pull the leg away from the body and slit the skin between the thigh and body. Bend back the leg until the thigh bone pops out of the hip joint. With the tip of the knife, cut through the broken joint, meat, and skin to sever the leg (hold the knife against the backbone as you cut). Repeat with the other leg.

STEP 2 SEPARATING LEGS

Place the leg skin side up on the cutting board. To find the joint, squeeze together the drum-stick and thigh; the flat, light-coloured area at the top is the joint. Cut through the joint to separate the drumstick and thigh into two pieces. Repeat with the other leg.

STEP 3 REMOVING WINGS

Pull the wing away from the body and slit the skin between the wing and body. Bend back the wing until the joint pops out. Cut through the broken joint, meat, and skin to sever the wing. Repeat with the other wing.

9

it is easiest to cut through the white cartilage where the ribs meet on the side

you may have to cut gently around the breastbone to release it

to skin chicken breasts, see page 10

STEP 4 SEPARATING BREAST FROM BODY

With poultry shears, kitchen scissors, or a sharp boning knife, sever the ribs between the breast and back. Cut from the cavity end toward the neck end on both sides. Bend the breast and back halves apart, exposing the joints at the neck that connect the two halves. Cut through the joints.

STEP 5 REMOVING BREASTBONE

With the breastbone facing you, use a small knife to slit open the membrane over the breastbone. Hold the breast at top and bottom and flex it up; the breastbone will pop out. Pull out the bone with your hand.

STEP 6 CUTTING BREAST IN HALF

Set the breast skin-side down. With a boning knife, cut down the centre of the breast along the groove left by the breastbone. You will now have two breast halves or fillets.

Steps in Skinning and Boning Chicken

BASIC TOOLS FOR SKINNING AND BONING

For skinning and boning, use a boning knife and kitchen scissors, plus a work surface that can be cleaned, like a resilient acrylic board.

BONING KNIFE

PARING KNIFE

ACRYLIC
CUTTING BOARD

KITCHEN SCISSORS

REMOVING THE BONES from chicken parts makes them cook faster; removing the skin allows direct browning of the surface of the meat. These steps prepare chicken parts for almost every cooking method used in this book: baking, barbecuing, grilling, sautéing, stir-frying, and braising. When you can do these steps yourself, you not only save money, you have more flexibility. Familiarity with these techniques means that you can buy a whole bird to cut up yourself as demonstrated on pages 8 and 9, then decide later whether to use the pieces with bones and/or skin intact or in a recipe that calls for boneless, skinless meat.

For breasts, deboning cuts away the breastbone and ribs. A boning knife is the best tool for this job, as its tapered, flexible blade slips easily between meat and bone. For thighs, which are smaller, use a boning knife or a small, sharp paring knife.

Stripping away skin is easily accomplished by hand, with the occasional assistance of a knife or kitchen scissors to release the skin from the meat.

if necessary, use a knife to cut the skin from the meat along the breastbone

STEP 1 SKINNING CHICKEN BREASTS OR THIGHS
Place a half breast skin-side up on a cutting board. Holding the piece with one hand, pull the skin away from the meat with the other hand, starting at the narrow end. Use the same technique for skinning chicken thighs.

10

gently pull the bones away from the meat as you work, so you can see the cutting area

removing the tough tendon makes the meat more tender and easier to flatten or roll up

STEP 2 BONING CHICKEN BREASTS

Starting at one side of the ribs, cut the meat away from the bones with a boning knife. Continue cutting, pressing the flat side of the knife blade almost flat against the rib bones. Cut as close to the bone as possible. One chicken yields two half-breast portions or fillets.

STEP 3 REMOVING TENDON FROM BREAST

To remove the tendon, pull it back with your fingers to stretch it out. With a knife, gently scrape the meat away from it until the entire length of the tendon is completely exposed. Sever and discard.

11

lift the bone by the upper end as you cut around it

cut skin away at the foot end of the leg if it doesn't pull off completely

the short side of the drumstick is on the inside of the leg

STEP 4 BONING CHICKEN THIGHS

Place the thigh on the cutting board with the meatier side down. With a boning knife or small, sharp knife, make a lengthwise slit through the meat to the bone. Carefully separate the meat from the bone by scraping it away around the bone and at the ends.

STEP 5 SKINNING DRUMSTICKS OR LEGS

With a pair of sharp kitchen scissors, slit the skin from the joint end to the foot end on the shortest side of the drumstick. Remove the skin by holding onto the meaty end and pulling toward the foot end.

Steps in Storing Chicken

CAREFUL HANDLING of raw poultry helps prevent transmittal of food-borne illness. To keep fresh poultry safe to eat, it must be properly stored in the refrigerator or freezer until you need it. Leftover cooked chicken and accompaniments like stuffing are equally susceptible to spoilage unless packaged and chilled as quickly as possible; never let them stand at room temperature for more than 2 hours.

Once purchased, store raw poultry in the coldest part of the refrigerator (not above 40°F/4°C) and use within 2 days. Cooked chicken, cut up or whole, should be used within 2 to 3 days. For longer storage, freeze a whole chicken for up to 1 year, chicken pieces for up to 6 months, and cooked chicken without sauce or liquid for up to 1 month. Never refrigerate or freeze a stuffed bird; always store stuffing separately. Frozen food keeps its quality at 0°F/minus 18°C or below, although some refrigerator-freezer compartments don't maintain this temperature. Check occasionally with a special freezer thermometer available in the kitchenware section of department stores, or from hardware shops.

The safest and best way to thaw frozen poultry is in the refrigerator. Allow 5 hours of thawing time per 1 lb/500 g. Poultry packaged in freezer wrap can be thawed under cold water in the sink or a large bowl; change the water every half hour (a 3-lb/1.5-kg chicken will be ready to cook in about 1½ hours). Defrosting at room temperature is not recommended because it creates a favourable environment for the growth of harmful organisms.

To avoid freezer burn — rough, dry areas where the meat has deteriorated from exposure to air — freeze poultry airtight and use within the suggested time limit.

Specially constructed heavy-duty polyethylene freezer bags and ties are stocked on most supermarket shelves, as are coated freezer paper sheets. Reusable freezer-safe plastic containers are another practical alternative. Always date each package to keep track of when to use it, and note the contents.

12

let the water run over the outside and through the inside of the bird

STEP 1 RINSING CHICKEN

Before cooking or freezing, a whole bird or chicken pieces should be rinsed and dried. Rinse under cold running water. Let excess water run off, then pat the chicken dry with paper towels.

seal tightly, pressing out as much air as possible

STEP 2 FREEZING CHICKEN

To freeze a whole chicken or chicken pieces, rinse and dry thoroughly, then place in a heavy-duty freezer bag, or wrap airtight in freezer paper. Label the contents, then date.

use a spoon or tongs, not fingers, for moving frozen meat from tray to storage container

When refrigerating or freezing uncooked or cooked chicken, package in sturdy bags or containers and date them.

STEP 3 FREEZING CUBED CHICKEN

Arrange leftover cooked cubed chicken on a tray in a single layer and freeze until firm. Transfer to freezer containers or freezer bags; label and date.

13

use heavy-duty containers or storage bags with a good seal

refrigerate leftovers or freeze them, as desired

STEP 4 REFRIGERATING STUFFING

After the meal, remove all stuffing from the bird and any remaining meat and store in separate containers. Never refrigerate or freeze stuffing in the bird.

Chicken Stock

Preparation Time: 30 minutes
Cooking Time: 2 hours

INGREDIENTS

3-1/2	LB/1.75 KG BONY CHICKEN PIECES (BONES, NECKS, AND WINGS FROM 3 CHICKENS)
3	STALKS CELERY WITH LEAVES, CUT UP
2	CARROTS, CUT UP
1	LARGE ONION, CUT UP
2	SPRIGS PARSLEY
1	TEASPOON SALT
1/2	TEASPOON DRIED THYME, SAGE, OR BASIL, CRUSHED
1/4	TEASPOON PEPPER
2	BAY LEAVES
48	FL OZ/1.5 L COLD WATER

*O*ne of the advantages of cutting up a whole chicken yourself is putting the leftover bony pieces to use in homemade chicken stock. Or purchase bones, necks, and wings from your supermarket.

■ In a large saucepan or boiler place chicken pieces, celery, carrots, onion, parsley, salt, thyme, sage, or basil, pepper, and bay leaves. Add water. Bring to boiling; reduce heat. Cover and simmer for 2 hours. Remove chicken.

■ To strain, pour stock through a large sieve or colander lined with 2 layers of pure cotton cheesecloth. Discard vegetables and seasonings. If using the stock while hot, skim fat. (Or chill the stock and lift off fat.)

■ If desired, when bones are cool enough to handle, remove meat from bones and reserve meat for another use. Discard bones. Store stock and reserved meat, if any, in separate covered containers in the refrigerator for up to 3 days or in the freezer for up to 6 months.

Makes about 40 fl oz/1.25 l stock and 15 oz/425 g meat

STEPS AT A GLANCE	Page
MAKING CHICKEN STOCK	14

STEPS IN MAKING CHICKEN STOCK

STEP 1 STRAINING STOCK

When the stock is done, remove from heat and lift out the chicken pieces with a slotted spoon or tongs. Pour stock through a large colander lined with 2 layers of pure cotton cheesecloth into a large bowl. Cool the chicken pieces and remove the meat from the bones, if desired.

STEP 2 REMOVING FAT

Let the stock cool briefly, then refrigerate for at least several hours or overnight. With a large spoon or wire skimmer, skim off and discard the fat that has hardened into a layer on the surface of the stock.

STEP 3 FREEZING STOCK

After the fat has been removed, transfer 8-fl oz/250-ml portions of stock to plastic freezer bags. Seal and date the bags, then lay them on their sides on a tray; freeze, remove from tray, and stack in the freezer until needed. Or, freeze small portions of stock in ice-cube trays, release the cubes, and store in labelled bags.

Roasting & Baking

Steps in Roasting Chicken

SHALLOW ROASTING PAN

BULB BASTER

PAPER TOWELS
AND ACRYLIC
CUTTING BOARD

BASIC TOOLS FOR ROASTING

You'll need kitchen string, scissors, a brush, bowls, and a cutting board for preparation; a roasting pan, a rack, and a bulb baster for cooking; paper towels and a thermometer to check doneness when roasting chicken.

TWO SMALL
GLASS BOWLS

STRING

STANDARD MEAT
THERMOMETER

INSTANT-READ
THERMOMETER

SOFT BRUSH

KITCHEN SCISSORS

16

WHO CAN RESIST a crisp, juicy roasted bird? As it cooks, it releases a wonderful aroma and a symphony of sizzles and crackles. This recipe for Basic Roast Chicken is one that you will serve with pleasure again and again.

Rinse and dry the bird (see page 12, step 1), then secure the legs and wings as shown on the opposite page. Season the skin and set on a rack in a roasting pan. To allow the underside to brown, it's best to elevate the bird on a rack so that it sits above the drippings.

The key to a perfectly roasted chicken is to cook it long enough so that it reaches a safe internal temperature (180°F/82.2°C in the thigh) yet is still moist and tender. Although a thermometer is the most accurate indicator, you can also judge doneness by jiggling the drumstick in its socket (it should move easily) and by piercing the thigh with a fork to check if the juices run clear and that there is no sign of pink in the meat.

BASIC ROAST CHICKEN

Preparation Time: 10 minutes
Roasting Time: 1¼ to 1½ hours

INGREDIENTS

1	3- TO 3-1/2-LB/1.5- TO 1.75-KG ROASTING CHICKEN
	COOKING OIL OR MELTED MARGARINE OR MELTED BUTTER
1-1/2	TABLESPOONS MIXED DRIED HERBS, SUCH AS SAGE, THYME, OREGANO, AND/OR ROSEMARY

■ Rinse chicken, then pat dry. Tie legs to tail; skewer neck skin to back; twist wings under the back. Brush bird with oil, margarine, or butter and season with herbs. Place bird, breast-side up, on a rack in a roasting pan. Roast in a preheated 375°F/190°C oven for 1¼ to 1½ hours, or till juices run clear and the drumsticks move easily in their sockets, spooning drippings over bird occasionally. Cover loosely with foil, then let stand 15 minutes before carving and serving.

Makes 6 servings

Per serving: 235 calories, 24 g protein, 0 g carbohydrate, 14 g total fat (4 g saturated), 79 mg cholesterol, 73 mg sodium, 200 mg potassium

use heavy-duty string
that won't burn at roasting
temperatures

the wing tips will
form a platform for
the bird to sit on

DONENESS TESTS

STEP 1 JIGGLING THE DRUMSTICK
To test for doneness, grasp the end of the drumstick with a paper towel. When it moves up and down and twists easily in its socket, the chicken is done.

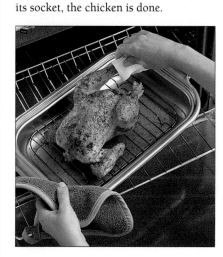

STEP 1 TYING DRUMSTICKS TO TAIL
Lay the bird, breast-side up, on the cutting board. Cut off a 12-in/30-cm length of kitchen string. Overlap the legs, then loop the string around the ends and the tail; pull tight to secure. Tie in a bow (the string will be cut away before the bird is carved and served).

STEP 2 TWISTING WINGS UNDER
Fasten the neck skin to the back with metal skewers or toothpicks. Pull the wings out, twist the tips under the bird, and push the wings in against the body.

17

be sure that the meat
thermometer does not
touch bone or the read-
ing will be too high

for flavour, sprinkle with
salt and pepper as well
as other seasonings

a baster with a metal tube
is preferable to a plastic
tube, which could melt from
the heat of the pan

STEP 3 RUBBING WITH SEASONINGS
Brush the entire bird with butter or oil as directed in the recipe. With your fingers, rub the seasonings onto the skin, then pat to adhere.

STEP 4 BASTING THE BIRD
To add flavour and moisture, and to encourage browning, use a bulb baster or large spoon to baste the chicken occasionally with pan juices as it roasts. Do this quickly, as the oven temperature drops each time the door is opened.

STEP 2 USING A THERMOMETER
Insert an instant-read thermometer into the centre of the inside thigh muscle (do not touch bone). The temperature should be 180°F/82°C. (Or a standard thermometer can be inserted into the bird before roasting; it stays in the bird until it's done.)

Steps in Carving Chicken

BASIC TOOLS FOR CARVING

For carving chicken, use a knife with a blade that can be sharpened, a sturdy oversized fork, and a carving board with a well for catching juices.

CARVING FORK

CARVING BOARD
WITH A WELL

CARVING KNIFE

O NCE THE ROAST CHICKEN is done, let it sit for about 15 minutes before carving, loosely covered with aluminium foil to retain heat. During this resting period the internal juices drawn to the surface recirculate throughout the bird and the flesh firms up. If the chicken is carved too soon, these juices will pour out onto the board, and the meat will be dry rather than moist and will shred when cut instead of slicing neatly.

Transfer the chicken to a grooved carving board and remove any stuffing to a serving dish. To carve, follow the basic steps shown on these two pages. Despite the mystique that surrounds it, carving is simple once you know where to cut — if you use the proper tools. A sharp carving knife and large, two-pronged fork are essential. Select a knife with a long, flexible blade made of a material that will take and maintain a sharp edge. If the blade is dull, it will hack apart even the most beautifully prepared bird and ruin its appearance. A dull knife also is more likely to slip and cut you. Use the fork to hold the bird steady as you work.

use a carving board that is big enough to hold the bird plus some of the carved pieces

to find the joint, pull the leg all the way down until the thigh joint pops out

STEP 1 CUTTING LEGS FROM ROAST CHICKEN
Set the fork in the centre of the chicken to keep it stable. Pull one leg away from the body and cut through the skin between the thigh and body with a sharp knife. Repeat on the other side.

STEP 2 CUTTING LEGS IN HALF

Place the leg, skin-side up, on the carving board. Cut through the joint between the drumstick and thigh to separate the leg into two pieces. Repeat with the other leg.

rather than cutting off each breast half in a single piece, you can carve away the meat in several slices directly from the bird

STEP 3 REMOVING BREAST MEAT

To remove a breast half in one whole piece, cut along one side of the breastbone and guide the knife down the rib bones, much as you would bone an uncooked breast (see page 11). Repeat with the second breast half.

if desired, remove the skin before slicing

STEP 4 SLICING BREAST MEAT

Once the breast halves are removed from the body, slice each into evenly thick pieces. If you cut across the grain of the meat, the slices will be more attractive.

STEP 5 REMOVING WINGS

As a final step, separate the wings from the body by cutting through the joints where the wing bones and backbone meet, as in removing the wings on an uncooked bird (see page 9).

Steps in Baking Boneless Chicken Breasts

BASIC TOOLS FOR BAKING BONELESS BREASTS

You'll need these basic tools to flatten, fill, and bake a stuffed boneless breast. A boning knife is used to bone the breasts.

BAKING DISH

SMALL BOWL

SPREADING KNIFE

MEAT
MALLET

BONING
KNIFE

SLICING KNIFE

PLASTIC WRAP AND
ACRYLIC CUTTING BOARD

THE MILD, JUICY GOODNESS of boned, skinned chicken breasts makes them the perfect starting point for a delicious baked main course. When pounded into evenly thick rectangles, they are an ideal base for tempting fillings like the seasoned caper and cream cheese mixture used on these pages (the recipe is on page 34). Rolled up and baked, then sliced and served with a tasty sauce, boneless breasts are succulent party fare. This cut of meat is so highly regarded that its classic culinary name is *suprême*.

The most perfect suprêmes are the ones you have trimmed yourself. Steps for skinning and boning chicken breasts are on page 10 and 11. Or you can have the butcher prepare them for you. Breasts to be filled will roll up more easily and cook more uniformly if they are first pounded with a metal meat mallet to square off their shape.

store the flattened chicken in the plastic wrap until ready to use

you can also place the chicken in a heavy-duty plastic bag and pound it

STEP 1 POUNDING CHICKEN BREASTS

Place each chicken breast half, boned-side up, between 2 pieces of plastic wrap. Working from the centre to the edges, pound with the flat side of a mallet to the desired thickness (a 1/8-in/3-mm-thick rectangle for stuffing).

leave enough bare space around
the edges so the meat can be
folded over the filling

STEP 2 PLACING FILLING ON BREASTS

Set the pounded breast halves on the work surface,
skinned-side down. With a small spatula or spoon,
spread an even layer of filling on each piece.

if the filling is not cheese,
butter, or anything that
melts, the sides *don't* need
to be tucked in

secure the rolls with
toothpicks, if necess-
ary, but remember to
remove them before
slicing and serving

STEP 3 ROLLING UP BREASTS

Fold the ends over the filling, then roll up like a jam roll,
starting from a long side. Brown the rolls, then transfer to
a baking dish and bake until tender and fully cooked.

21

another way to test for
doneness is to see if the
meat juices run clear

STEP 4 TESTING FOR DONENESS

After the stuffed rolls have cooked, remove the baking
dish from the oven onto a rack or trivet. Slice into a
roll. If no pink remains, the chicken is done. Set the
rolls on a board and slice.

Stuffed boneless breasts (page 34)
make an impressive yet easy-to-
prepare centrepiece for any meal.

Roast Chicken with Pecan Rice Stuffing

Preparation Time: 30 minutes
Roasting Time: 1¼ to 1½ hours

INGREDIENTS

7	OZ/220 G WILD PECAN RICE OR BROWN LONG GRAIN RICE
	CHICKEN STOCK
2-1/2	OZ/75 G CHOPPED FRESH FENNEL BULB
3/4	OZ/20 G CHOPPED SPRING ONION
1	TABLESPOON MARGARINE OR BUTTER
2	OZ/60 G PECANS (OPTIONAL)
1-1/2	OZ/45 G DRIED CRANBERRIES OR DRIED TART RED CHERRIES OR DRIED CURRANTS
1/2	OZ/15 G CHOPPED FRESH PARSLEY
1	3- TO 3-1/2-LB/1.5- TO 1.75-KG ROASTING CHICKEN
1	TABLESPOON COOKING OIL, OR MARGARINE OR BUTTER, MELTED

If you can't find wild pecan rice use long grain brown rice instead and add pecans to the stuffing to give it a nutty flavor.

■ Prepare pecan rice according to package directions, except use chicken stock in place of water and omit salt. Or, bring 16 fl oz/500 ml of stock to boiling, add the brown rice, and cook, covered, for about 20 minutes, or till rice is tender and liquid is absorbed. Set aside.

■ Meanwhile, in a medium frying pan cook fennel and spring onion in 1 tablespoon margarine or butter till tender. Stir in pecans (if using), cranberries, cherries or currants, and parsley; heat through. Stir into cooked rice.

■ Rinse chicken; pat dry. Spoon some of the stuffing loosely into the neck cavity; skewer neck skin to back. Lightly spoon stuffing into the body cavity. (Put any remaining stuffing into a 1-qt/1-l casserole. Bake the stuffing in the casserole, covered, for 30 to 35 minutes while chicken is cooking.)

■ Tie the drumsticks securely to tail. Twist the wing tips under the back. Place the chicken, breast-side up, on a rack in a shallow roasting pan. Brush the chicken with cooking oil, margarine, or butter. Roast, uncovered, in a preheated 375°F/190°C oven for 1¼ to 1½ hours, or till juices run clear and the drumsticks move easily in their sockets. Cover loosely with foil and let stand for 15 minutes before carving.

Makes 6 servings

Per serving: 391 calories, 29 g protein, 31 g carbohydrate, 16 g total fat (4 g saturated), 79 mg cholesterol, 362 mg sodium, 358 mg potassium

STEPS AT A GLANCE	Page
STUFFING CHICKEN	22
ROASTING CHICKEN	16
CARVING CHICKEN	18

22

STEPS IN STUFFING CHICKEN

STEP 1 SKEWERING NECK
Loosely fill the neck cavity with prepared rice stuffing. Close off by pulling the neck skin over the opening and securing it to the back with a small metal skewer.

STEP 2 STUFFING BODY
Spoon the stuffing into the body cavity. Fill the cavity, but don't pack it with stuffing, as the mixture will expand during roasting. When the drumsticks are tied together, they will cover the exposed stuffing.

For a spectacular presentation, place a
whole roast chicken on a large platter and
garnish with fresh herbs, orange slices, and grapes.
Carve at the table and serve extra stuffing with the bird.

Chicken with Lemon Stuffing

STEPS AT A GLANCE	Page
STUFFING CHICKEN	22
ROASTING CHICKEN	16
CARVING CHICKEN	18
MAKING GRAVY	24

Preparation Time: 35 minutes
Roasting Time: 1¼ to 1½ hours

INGREDIENTS

STUFFING

14	OZ/440 G DRY BREAD CUBES
2-1/2	OZ/75 G FINELY CHOPPED ONION
2	TEASPOONS FINELY SHREDDED LEMON PEEL
1/2	TEASPOON DRIED MARJORAM, CRUSHED
1/2	TEASPOON DRIED THYME, CRUSHED
1/4	TEASPOON SALT
1/4	TEASPOON PEPPER
1	CLOVE GARLIC, MINCED
1	LIGHTLY BEATEN EGG
4	OZ/125 G MARGARINE OR BUTTER, MELTED
3	TABLESPOONS WATER
2	TABLESPOONS LEMON JUICE

ROAST CHICKEN

1	3- TO 3-1/2-LB/1.5- TO 1.75-KG ROASTING CHICKEN
1	TABLESPOON COOKING OIL, OR MARGARINE OR BUTTER, MELTED

PAN GRAVY

2	FL OZ/60 ML RESERVED FAT SKIMMED FROM PAN DRIPPINGS
	SKIMMED PAN DRIPPINGS
1	OZ/30 G PLAIN FLOUR
	CHICKEN STOCK OR WATER
1/2	TEASPOON FINELY SHREDDED LEMON PEEL
	SALT
	PEPPER

*F*resh lemon juice and herbs invigorate the flavour of the stuffing in this simple roast chicken. Drizzle the extra stuffing with water before baking to help keep it moist; you can also use chicken stock or white wine for this purpose.*

■ For stuffing, in a mixing bowl stir together the bread cubes, onion, lemon peel, marjoram, thyme, salt, pepper, and garlic. In another bowl stir together the egg, melted margarine or butter, water, and lemon juice. Drizzle over the bread cubes; toss to mix.

■ For roast chicken, rinse chicken and pat dry. Spoon some of the stuffing loosely into the neck cavity; skewer neck skin to back. Lightly spoon stuffing into the body cavity. (Put any remaining stuffing into a 1-qt/1-l casserole. Drizzle with 1 to 2 tablespoons additional water. Bake, covered, for 20 to 30 minutes while the chicken is cooking.) Tie the drumsticks securely to tail. Twist the wing tips under the back. Place the chicken, breast-side up, on a rack in a shallow roasting pan. Brush the chicken with oil, margarine, or butter. Roast, uncovered, in a preheated 375°F/190°C oven for 1¼ to 1½ hours, or till juices run clear and the drumsticks move easily in their sockets. Cover with foil and let stand for 15 minutes before carving.

■ For pan gravy, pour pan drippings from roast chicken into a large measuring cup. Also scrape the browned bits from the bottom of the pan into the cup. Skim and reserve fat from drippings. Return 2 fl oz/60 ml of the fat to the roasting pan (discard remaining fat). Stir in flour and cook till bubbly. Add enough stock or water to remaining drippings in the measuring cup to equal 16 fl oz/500 ml. Add all at once to flour mixture. Cook and stir over medium heat till thickened. Add lemon peel. Season to taste with salt and pepper.

Makes 6 servings

Per serving: 598 calories, 31 g protein, 25 g carbohydrate, 41 g total fat (10 g saturated), 122 mg cholesterol, 834 mg sodium, 367 mg potassium

STEPS IN MAKING GRAVY

STEP 1 COOKING FLOUR
Pour 2 fl oz/60 ml reserved fat, skimmed from the drippings, into the roasting pan. Sprinkle the flour over the fat while stirring; cook till bubbly.

STEP 2 THICKENING GRAVY
Add enough stock or water to the remaining drippings to make 16 fl oz/500 ml liquid, then pour into the flour mixture. Cook over medium heat, stirring constantly, until thickened.

24

Tender, juicy slices of roast chicken team up with stuffing, steamed asparagus and carrots for an appealing main course. Pan gravy is spooned over each portion.

Seasoned under the skin, then roasted to crispy
perfection, this glorious bird looks dramatic
on a platter garnished with fresh chilies
and coriander sprigs.

Roast Chicken with Chili-Coriander Butter

*B*ecause *chilies contain volatile oils that can burn skin and eyes, avoid direct contact with them as much as possible. Wear clear plastic bags or plastic or rubber gloves on your hands to protect your skin from the oils in the chilies. Avoid any contact with your eyes. Wash your hands and nails thoroughly with soap and water when finished. Chinese parsley, or fresh coriander, is the leafy part of the coriander plant that also gives us coriander seed.*

■ In a food processor bowl or blender container finely chop the garlic cloves and red chilies. (Keep lid closed while processing and open lid carefully, being careful not to inhale directly over bowl.) Add butter or margarine and coriander; process or blend till nearly smooth.

■ Beginning at the neck of the bird, loosen the skin from the breast by working your fingers and thumb toward the tail. Loosen as much skin as possible without piercing the skin. Turn over and continue to loosen skin down both sides of the backbone, thighs, and legs. Spread the butter mixture, 1 tablespoon at a time, under the skin on the chicken breast and back. Rub your thumb on top of the skin to distribute the butter mixture under the skin as evenly as possible.

■ Tie legs to tail; pull neck skin to back and skewer. Twist wing tips under back. Sprinkle chicken with paprika and onion salt. Place bird, breast-side up, on a rack in a shallow roasting pan. Roast, uncovered, in a preheated 375°F/190°C oven for 1¼ to 1½ hours, or till juices run clear and drumsticks move easily in their sockets. Cover loosely with foil and let stand for 15 minutes before carving.

Makes 6 servings

Per serving: 289 calories, 25 g protein, 1 g carbohydrate, 20 g total fat (5 g saturated), 79 mg cholesterol, 231 mg sodium, 249 mg potassium

STEPS AT A GLANCE	Page
SEASONING CHICKEN UNDER THE SKIN	27
ROASTING CHICKEN	16
CARVING CHICKEN	18

Preparation Time: 25 minutes
Roasting Time: 1¼ to 1½ hours

INGREDIENTS

4	CLOVES GARLIC, PEELED
2	FRESH RED CHILIES, STEMMED, CORED, SEEDED, AND COARSELY CHOPPED
2	OZ/60 G BUTTER *OR* MARGARINE, CUT INTO 4 PIECES
1	CUP FRESH CORIANDER (CHINESE PARSLEY)
1	3- TO 3-1/2-LB/1.5- TO 1.75-KG ROASTING CHICKEN
	PAPRIKA
	ONION SALT

27

STEPS IN SEASONING CHICKEN UNDER THE SKIN

STEP 1 LOOSENING SKIN
Beginning at the neck end of the bird, work your hand under the skin to loosen it. Start over the breast first, from the neck toward the tail. Then continue down both sides of the backbone to the thighs, and legs. Be careful not to pierce the skin.

STEP 2 DISTRIBUTING BUTTER
Put 1 tablespoon of the butter mixture at a time under the skin at the breast and back. With a sliding motion, distribute the butter with your thumb as evenly as possible.

Roast Chicken with Minted Spice Rub

*T*he combination of spices has a Middle Eastern flair and forms a wonderfully flavourful, crunchy crust. Sprinkle the cavity of the chicken with any leftover spices.

■ Rinse chicken; pat dry. In a small mixing bowl stir together the dried mint, cardamom, cinnamon, salt, and pepper. Brush chicken with oil, then rub mint-spice mixture onto the skin. Skewer neck skin to back, tie legs to tail, and twist wing tips under back.

■ Place bird, breast-side up, on a rack in a shallow roasting pan. Roast, uncovered, in a preheated 375°F/190°C oven for 1¼ to 1½ hours, or till juices run clear and drumsticks move easily in their sockets. Cover loosely with foil, then let stand for 15 minutes before carving. If desired, garnish with fresh mint leaves.

Makes 6 servings

Per serving: 237 calories, 25 g protein, 0 g carbohydrate, 15 g total fat (4 g saturated), 79 mg cholesterol, 264 mg sodium, 208 mg potassium

INGREDIENTS

1	3- TO 3-1/2-LB/1- TO 1.75-KG ROASTING CHICKEN
2	TEASPOONS DRIED MINT LEAVES, CRUSHED
1	TEASPOON GROUND CARDAMOM
1/2	TEASPOON GROUND CINNAMON
1/2	TEASPOON SALT
1/4	TEASPOON PEPPER
1	TABLESPOON COOKING OIL *OR* OLIVE OIL
	FRESH MINT LEAVES (OPTIONAL)

Preparation Time: 15 minutes
Roasting Time: 1¼ to 1½ hours

STEPS AT A GLANCE	Page
ROASTING CHICKEN	16
CARVING CHICKEN	18

28

Sautéed zucchini (courgettes), and couscous mixed with peas and diced carrots, complement the earthy spices used on this roasted bird.

Chicken with Roasted Garlic Sauce

INGREDIENTS

Preparation Time: 30 minutes
Roasting Time: 1¼ to 1½ hours

1	3- TO 3-1/2-LB/1.5- TO 1.75-KG ROASTING CHICKEN
15	CLOVES GARLIC, PEELED
1	TABLESPOON MINCED GARLIC (ABOUT 6 CLOVES)
1	TEASPOON SALT
1	TABLESPOON COOKING OIL
3	FL OZ/250 ML WATER
1	OZ/30 G PLAIN FLOUR
	CHICKEN STOCK
1	TABLESPOON LEMON JUICE
	PEPPER
	CHOPPED FRESH PARSLEY (OPTIONAL)

*W*hile raw garlic is potent and sharp, when oven-roasted it takes on a mellow, delicate sweetness.

■ Rinse chicken; pat dry. Flatten 5 of the garlic cloves and place inside the body cavity of chicken. Skewer neck skin to back; tie legs to tail. Twist wings under back. Combine the minced garlic and salt. Brush chicken with oil, then rub garlic-salt mixture onto the skin.

■ Place chicken, breast-side up, on a rack in a shallow roasting pan. In another ovenproof pan combine remaining garlic cloves and the water. Place both pans in a preheated 375°F/190°C oven and roast, uncovered, for 1¼ to 1½ hours, or till juices run clear and the drumsticks move easily in their sockets. Spoon drippings over chicken occasionally. If necessary, cover chicken with foil for the last 20 minutes of roasting to prevent overbrowning. Check garlic cloves to be sure they have enough water to cook gently, but not burn. Transfer chicken to a serving platter. Let stand, covered loosely with foil, for 15 minutes before carving.

■ Meanwhile, pour pan drippings into a large measuring cup. Also scrape browned bits into the cup. Skim and reserve fat from drippings. Place 2 fl oz/60 ml of the fat into a medium saucepan (discard remaining fat). Stir in flour; cook and stir for 2 minutes, or till flour is golden. To the remaining drippings in measuring cup, add the cooked garlic cloves and their cooking water and enough chicken stock to equal 16 fl oz/500 ml. Add all at once to flour mixture. Cook and stir over medium heat till thickened and bubbly. Cook and stir for 2 minutes more. Stir in lemon juice and season to taste with pepper. If desired, garnish with parsley.

Makes 6 servings

Per serving: 472 calories, 31 g protein, 27 g carbohydrate, 26 g total fat (7 g saturated), 87 mg cholesterol, 685 mg sodium, 367 mg potassium

Emphasise the country flavours of this mild garlic chicken by serving it with pasta bows, cooked carrots, and baguette slices.

STEPS AT A GLANCE	Page
ROASTING CHICKEN	16
CARVING CHICKEN	18
MAKING GRAVY	24

Poussins Roasted with Vegetable Stuffing

Preparation Time: 30 minutes
Roasting Time: 1¼ to 1½ hours

STEPS AT A GLANCE	Page
STUFFING CHICKEN	22
ROASTING CHICKEN	16

30

INGREDIENTS

5	OZ/155 G FINELY CHOPPED CARROTS
5	OZ/155 G FINELY CHOPPED CELERY
1-1/2	OZ/45 G FINELY CHOPPED LEEK
1-1/2	OZ/45 G SLICED FRESH MUSHROOMS
2-1/2	OZ/75 G FINELY CHOPPED ONION
2	TABLESPOONS MARGARINE OR BUTTER
1/2	TEASPOON DRIED THYME, CRUSHED
1/2	TEASPOON SALT
1/4	TEASPOON PEPPER
2	FL OZ/60 ML HEAVY (DOUBLE) CREAM (OPTIONAL)
2	1- TO 1-1/2-LB/500- TO 750-G POUSSINS OR CORNISH GAME HENS
1	TABLESPOON COOKING OIL

*U*se either poussins or Cornish game hens to make this country-style dish. If you prefer, roast 4 poussins and serve a whole bird to each person.

Bake a few quartered red potatoes in oil in the same oven as the poussins for an easy accompaniment.

■ In a large frying pan cook carrots, celery, leek, mushrooms, and onion in hot margarine or butter for about 5 minutes, or till vegetables are crisp-tender, but not brown. Add thyme, salt, and pepper. If desired, stir in cream to moisten. Cool vegetable mixture slightly.

■ Rinse birds; pat dry. Spoon some of the vegetable mixture loosely into the body cavity of each bird. Pull neck skin, if present, to back of each bird. Twist wing tips under back. Tie legs to tail. Put any remaining stuffing into a small casserole; cover and chill. Place the birds, breast-sides up, on a rack in a shallow roasting pan. Brush birds with cooking oil. Cover loosely with foil. Bake in a preheated 375°F/190°C oven for 45 minutes. Uncover birds. Bake 30 to 45 minutes more, or till juices run clear and the drumsticks move easily in their sockets. Add stuffing to oven the last 20 minutes of roasting. Let birds stand, covered loosely with foil, for 15 minutes before serving. To serve, cut each bird in half. Serve with stuffing.

Makes 4 servings

Per serving: 375 calories, 31 g protein, 9 g carbohydrate, 25 g total fat (8 g saturated), 115 mg cholesterol, 475 mg sodium, 254 mg potassium

Poussins with Cherry Sauce

*P*oussins are simple to prepare and make an impressive main course. For an attractive appearance, surround the birds with whole sprigs of fresh rosemary or thyme and sprinkle them with shredded orange peel.

■ Halve the birds and place cut-side down on a rack in a roasting pan. Brush birds with cooking oil; sprinkle with salt and pepper. Bake, uncovered, in a preheated 375°F/190°C oven for 1 to 1½ hours, or till juices run clear.

■ Meanwhile, in a small saucepan melt the jam over low heat. Stir together the vinegar, orange juice concentrate, kirsch (if desired), water, and cornflour. Add to saucepan. Cook and stir over medium heat till thickened and bubbly. Cook and stir for 2 minutes more. Serve sauce with birds.

Makes 4 servings

Per serving: 463 calories, 30 g protein, 45 g carbohydrate, 19 g total fat (4 g saturated), 100 mg cholesterol, 83 mg sodium, 86 mg potassium

INGREDIENTS

2	1- TO 1-1/2-LB/500- TO 750-G POUSSINS OR CORNISH GAME HENS
2	TEASPOONS COOKING OIL
1/8	TEASPOON SALT
1/8	TEASPOON PEPPER
7-1/2	OZ/240 G CHERRY JAM
1	TABLESPOON CIDER VINEGAR
1	TABLESPOON FROZEN ORANGE JUICE CONCENTRATE, THAWED
1	TABLESPOON KIRSCH (OPTIONAL)
1	TABLESPOON WATER
2	TEASPOONS CORNFLOUR

Preparation Time: 20 minutes
Roasting Time: 1 to 1½ hours

STEPS AT A GLANCE	Page
ROASTING CHICKEN	16

The combination of fruit-based sauces and game birds has variations in cuisines around the world. This version combines cherries with poussins to appeal to modern tastes.

31

Carolina-Style Oven-barbecued Chicken

Try a scoop of coleslaw with these spicy filled rolls. It's not only a terrific flavour combination, but the coleslaw will cool hot tongues as well.

Preparation Time: 25 minutes
Baking Time: 45 minutes

INGREDIENTS

1	TEASPOON SUGAR
1	TEASPOON GARLIC POWDER
1	TEASPOON PAPRIKA
1/2	TEASPOON GROUND ALLSPICE
1/2	TEASPOON BLACK PEPPER
1/4	TEASPOON SALT
1/4	TEASPOON DRY MUSTARD POWDER
1/8	TEASPOON GROUND RED (CAYENNE) PEPPER
4	WHOLE CHICKEN LEGS, SKINNED (ABOUT 2-1/2 LB/1.25 KG)
2	TABLESPOONS VINEGAR
2	TABLESPOONS WATER
1	TABLESPOON HONEY
1	TEASPOON WORCESTERSHIRE SAUCE
1/2	TO 1 TEASPOON BOTTLED HOT CHILI SAUCE
1/2	TEASPOON PREPARED MUSTARD
6	HAMBURGER BUNS, SPLIT AND TOASTED

*T*o *approximate the slow-cooked, vinegary taste of barbecued chicken as it's served in the southern states of America, roast chicken legs, then shred the meat, and mix it with a pungent sauce.*

STEPS AT A GLANCE	Page
SKINNING DRUMSTICKS OR LEGS	11
ROASTING CHICKEN	16
SHREDDING COOKED CHICKEN	109

■ In a small mixing bowl combine sugar, garlic powder, paprika, allspice, black pepper, salt, dry mustard, and ground red pepper. Rub spice mixture onto chicken legs. Place chicken on a rack in a shallow roasting pan. Bake, uncovered, in a preheated 375°F/190°C oven for 45 minutes, or till chicken is tender and no longer pink. Cool chicken slightly. Remove chicken meat from bones; shred meat.

■ In a medium saucepan combine vinegar, water, honey, Worcestershire sauce, hot chili sauce, and prepared mustard. Stir in shredded chicken; heat through. Serve in hamburger buns.

Makes 6 servings

Per serving: 282 calories, 25 g protein, 25 g carbohydrate, 9 g total fat (2 g saturated), 73 mg cholesterol, 423 mg sodium, 250 mg potassium

32

Smoky Chicken Wings

STEPS AT A GLANCE	Page
REMOVING WINGS	9

Preparation Time: 15 minutes
Marinating Time: 1 hour
Baking Time: 30 to 35 minutes

INGREDIENTS

8	FL OZ/250 ML WATER
3	FL OZ/80 ML LIQUID SMOKE
2	TABLESPOONS WORCESTERSHIRE SAUCE
3	TABLESPOONS DRIED PARSLEY FLAKES
1-1/2	TEASPOONS DRIED OREGANO, CRUSHED
1-1/2	TEASPOONS PAPRIKA
3/4	TEASPOON GARLIC POWDER
3/4	TEASPOON SALT
3/4	TEASPOON PEPPER
16	CHICKEN WINGS (ABOUT 3 LB/1.5 KG)

*S*erve these pungent wings whole as a main course. Or, to serve them as hors d'oeuvres, remove tips and cut wings in half at the joint so they can be easily handled. Liquid smoke (hickory oil) is available at gourmet grocers and delicatessens.

■ In a medium mixing bowl combine water, liquid smoke, Worcestershire sauce, parsley flakes, oregano, paprika, garlic powder, salt, and pepper. Place chicken wings or pieces in a plastic bag set in a shallow dish. Pour marinade over chicken in bag. Seal bag and turn to coat chicken wings or pieces well.

■ Marinate in the refrigerator for about 1 hour, turning bag once. Remove chicken from bag; discard marinade. Place chicken wings or pieces on a foil-lined baking sheet or shallow baking pan. Bake in a preheated 400°F/200°C oven for 30 to 35 minutes, or till chicken is tender and no longer pink.

Makes 4 servings

Per serving: 448 calories, 41 g protein, 1 g carbohydrate, 30 g total fat (8 g saturated), 131 mg cholesterol, 364 mg sodium, 296 mg potassium

Piled high on a festive platter, these baked chicken wings are impossible to resist.

Stuffed Chicken Breasts with Red Pepper Coulis

STEPS AT A GLANCE	Page
SKINNING & BONING CHICKEN	10
BAKING BONELESS CHICKEN BREASTS	20

Preparation Time: 25 minutes
Baking Time: 20 to 25 minutes

INGREDIENTS

STUFFED CHICKEN BREASTS

3	OZ/90 G PACKAGED CREAM CHEESE, SOFTENED
2	TABLESPOONS GRATED PARMESAN CHEESE
1	TABLESPOON DRAINED CAPERS
1	TABLESPOON MILK
1	CLOVE GARLIC, MINCED
	DASH PEPPER
4	BONELESS, SKINLESS CHICKEN BREAST HALVES (1 LB/500 G TOTAL)
1	TABLESPOON OLIVE OIL *OR* COOKING OIL
2	FL OZ/60 ML DRY WHITE WINE

RED PEPPER COULIS

2	MEDIUM-SIZED RED PEPPERS (CAPSICUMS), ROASTED AND PEELED, *OR* 5 OZ/155 G BOTTLED ROASTED PEPPERS, DRAINED
1	TABLESPOON OLIVE OIL *OR* COOKING OIL
2	CLOVES GARLIC, MINCED
2	FL OZ/60 ML LIGHT (SINGLE) CREAM
2	TEASPOONS ANCHOVY PASTE
1	TABLESPOON DRAINED CAPERS

34

*T*he pepper coulis, or puréed sauce, makes a colourful background for chicken. Add even more vibrancy by garnishing the plates with a fresh herb sprig or swirling a bit of sour cream through the sauce with a toothpick.

■ For stuffed chicken breasts, in a small mixing bowl combine cream cheese, Parmesan cheese, capers, milk, garlic, and pepper; set aside.

■ Rinse chicken; pat dry. Place each breast half between 2 pieces of plastic wrap. Working from the centre to the edges, pound chicken lightly with the flat side of a meat mallet to a ⅛-in/3-mm thickness. Remove plastic wrap. Spread one quarter of the cream cheese mixture over each breast half. Fold in the sides and roll up jam-roll style, pressing the edges to seal. In a large frying pan heat olive oil or cooking oil. Brown chicken on both sides (about 5 minutes total). Transfer chicken to a 2-qt/2-l baking dish. Pour wine over chicken. Bake, uncovered, in a preheated 350°F/180°C oven for 20 to 25 minutes, or till chicken is tender and no pink remains.

■ Meanwhile, for red pepper coulis, in a blender container or food processor bowl blend or process roasted peppers till smooth; set aside. In a small saucepan heat remaining olive oil or cooking oil. Add garlic; cook and stir till tender but not brown. Add puréed roasted pepper, light cream, anchovy paste, and 1 tablespoon capers. Heat through. To serve, spoon coulis onto 4 dinner plates and top with sliced chicken breasts.

Makes 4 servings

Per serving: 297 calories, 22 g protein, 4 g carbohydrate, 20 g total fat (8 g saturated), 80 mg cholesterol, 423 mg sodium, 289 mg potassium

For an elegant appearance, arrange slices of stuffed chicken breasts in a pinwheel pattern on top of the sauce; decorate with clusters of asparagus tips and shredded lemon peel.

Grilling & Barbecuing

Steps in Grilling Chicken

Use a grill pan with a slotted rack, a ruler to measure the distance between the heating element and the food's surface, and a cup and brush for basting.

GRILL PAN WITH RACK

MEASURING
CUP

PASTRY BRUSH

RULER

36

BARBECUING AND GRILLING are basic methods that are well suited to cooking chicken because they show off its wonderful versatility. In essence, they are identical techniques. While barbecuing is usually done out of doors and grilling in the kitchen, both utilise dry, radiant heat that first quickly hits the surface of chicken and then slowly travels through the meat until it has penetrated to its centre. The main difference is that in most cases the heat in grilling comes from the top while in barbecuing it comes from beneath.

In some ways, grilling is even simpler than barbecuing because it requires no special equipment other than a grill pan with a rack, and because a grill is built into most home stoves. For grilling, however, as with barbecuing, a delicate balance of time and distance from the heat must be coordinated to produce a deliciously juicy end result: food that is nicely browned on the outside and properly cooked within. The trick is to know how far away from the heating element to set the oven rack and grill pan. As a rule, because they take longer to cook

through, thicker pieces with bones need more distance, about 5 to 6 in/13 to 15 cm, than quick-cooking boneless cuts or kebabs, which should be cooked about 4 in/10 cm from the heat.

Most oven manufacturers provide a grill pan. If you must purchase one, the rack should be slotted so that grease drips into the pan below. That way the food doesn't sit in its fat and there is less chance of flareups. For easier cleaning, you may want to line the pan with aluminium foil, although those with a nonstick surface wipe clean with little effort. Don't wrap the rack with foil, though, or the fat won't drain.

Grilling poultry is often a good choice for low-fat diets. But unlike barbecuing, grilling imparts no flavour of its own to food. Some seasoning, in the form of herbs, a marinade, or a baste, is required to transform what could be a bland dish into one that is full of flavour. The recipes in this chapter will introduce you to the wonderful variety that is possible when you cook chicken under the grill or on the barbecue.

try to grill chicken pieces that are similar in size so that they cook in the same amount of time

pull the oven rack with the grill pan out of the oven when basting to keep your hands safe from the heat

baste evenly, saving some of the sauce to brush on just before serving, if desired

STEP 1 ARRANGING CHICKEN ON PAN

If chicken pieces have been marinated, lift them from marinade and drain slightly. Arrange the chicken pieces skin-side down on the unheated grill rack, then set the pan on the oven rack.

STEP 2 MEASURING DISTANCE FROM HEAT

Always measure from the heating element to the surface of the food. Most cuts should be grilled 4 to 6 in/10 to 15 cm from the heat; adjust the height of the oven rack, if necessary. Preheat the grill according to manufacturer's directions.

STEP 3 BASTING CHICKEN

Grill the chicken completely on its underside before basting. Turn the pieces with long-handled tongs to protect your hands, then brush with the marinade or glaze as directed in the recipe.

37

Brush on a simple sauce or marinade, such as the honey-soy glaze on page 45, and the flavour of grilled chicken changes dramatically.

Steps in Barbecuing Chicken

DRIP PAN

CHARCOAL

LONG TONGS

BASTING BRUSH

BASIC TOOLS FOR BARBECUING

Light the barbecue with barbecue charcoal and long matches; use long-handled tongs and a basting brush to keep your hands away from the fire. A drip pan is used for indirect-heat barbecuing.

LONG MATCHES

CHICKEN IS IDEAL for barbecuing. We never tire of the smoky essence that infuses its mild-flavoured meat or of the wonderful aroma as it finishes to a crispy turn before our eyes. Chicken cooked over hot coals is not only exceptionally flavourful, but it also suits today's health-conscious cooking because barbecuing is a dry-heat method that requires very little added fat.

Whether you use a simple grate set across a pile of rocks or an elaborate barbecue, the goal is the same: to balance time and temperature so that the food is moist and tender. But a good barbecue cook also depends on visual clues: Is the food cooking evenly? Should it be turned so it won't burn? Barbecuing is very interactive; it requires your attention. That's what makes it fun to do and to watch.

The steps on these pages demonstrate how to start a charcoal fire correctly for both direct- and indirect-heat cooking. Your recipe will specify which method to use. Always preheat the upper cooking rack over the ash-grey coals for a few minutes and brush it with oil so food won't stick to it. Afterwards, scrape it clean with a wire brush for the same reason.

Barbecue recipes in this book are also suitable for gas barbecues. The same temperatures should be used for both charcoal and gas barbecues.

use enough charcoal so that when spread out in a single layer, it will extend slightly beyond the cooking area

the charcoal is ready when covered with a grey ash: 30 to 40 minutes for ordinary charcoal, 5 to 10 minutes for self-lighting

STEP 1 LIGHTING CHARCOAL

Arrange the barbecue charcoal in a pyramid in the centre of the lower grate. If it is self-lighting, ignite with a match. If not, use an electric starter or fire lighter.

use the direct-heat method for barbecuing smaller chicken pieces

use the indirect-heat method for barbecuing whole chicken

hold your hand in the centre of the barbecue above the coals or pan

STEP 2 **CHARCOAL FOR DIRECT HEAT**

For direct-heat barbecuing, use long-handled tongs and spread the hot coals in a single layer across the grate. Food will cook more evenly if the coals are arranged with about ½ in/12 mm of space between each piece.

STEP 3 **CHARCOAL FOR INDIRECT HEAT**

For indirect-heat barbecuing, arrange the hot coals around the edge of the grate, leaving a space in the centre. Set a disposable foil drip pan in the middle so that it is surrounded by charcoal. The food is placed on the upper cooking rack over the drip pan, then the barbecue is covered so that heat and smoke circulate evenly.

STEP 4 **TESTING HEAT OF COALS**

Check the temperature by holding your hand, palm-side down, at about the height at which the food will cook. If you must pull your hand away after 2 seconds, the coals are hot; 3 seconds, medium hot; 4 seconds, medium; 5 seconds, medium slow; 6 seconds, slow. When barbecuing with indirect heat, the temperature of the coals should be one level hotter than the desired temperature over the drip pan.

39

STEP 5 **BRUSHING MEAT WITH MARINADE**

Use a long-handled basting brush to coat the chicken with marinade. Marinades containing raw meat juices should be thoroughly cooked on the meat, so be sure to cook the chicken at least 5 minutes more after the last time you brush it with the marinade. Or, cook the marinade by bringing it to boiling before brushing onto the meat.

Golden-brown, juicy chicken pieces soaked in the same tangy citrus marinade used for a butterflied chicken (page 43) are barbecued for a light main course or lunch dish.

Chicken Breasts with Tomato-Mint Pesto

Preparation Time: 20 minutes
Grilling Time: 25 to 35 minutes

INGREDIENTS

1/2	OZ/15 G PACKED FRESH MINT LEAVES
1/2	OZ/15 G PACKED FRESH PARSLEY SPRIGS WITH STEMS REMOVED
1	OZ/30 G DRIED TOMATOES
2	FL OZ/60 ML OLIVE OIL
1	CLOVE GARLIC, HALVED
1-1/2	TEASPOONS FINELY SHREDDED LEMON PEEL
1/4	TEASPOON SALT
1/8	TEASPOON LEMON-PEPPER SEASONING
4	MEDIUM CHICKEN BREAST HALVES (1 LB/500 G TOTAL)

F or a more Italian flavour, omit the lemon pepper and use fresh basil leaves instead of the mint. This pesto is also a tasty accompaniment to lamb or pork.

■ In a blender container or food processor bowl combine mint leaves, parsley, dried tomatoes, olive oil, garlic, lemon peel, salt, and lemon-pepper seasoning. Cover and blend or process till finely chopped. Set aside.

■ If desired, remove skin from chicken. Cut a pocket in each chicken breast half by cutting a 2-in/5-cm-deep slit just above the breastbone on the meaty side of the breast. Fill each pocket with one quarter of the pesto.

■ Place breasts, bone-side up, on the unheated rack of the grill pan. Grill 4 to 5 in/10 to 13 cm from the heat for 20 minutes. Turn chicken and grill 5 to 15 minutes more, or till tender and no pink remains.

Makes 4 servings

Per serving: 328 calories, 29 g protein, 6 g carbohydrate, 21 g total fat (4 g saturated), 78 mg cholesterol, 254 mg sodium, 402 mg potassium

STEPS AT A GLANCE	Page
MAKING POCKETS	40
GRILLING CHICKEN	36

STEPS IN MAKING POCKETS

STEP 1 CUTTING POCKETS

Place a chicken breast half on the cutting board skin-side up. With a small knife or boning knife, make a pocket 2 in/5 cm deep and about 3 in/7.5 cm long in the breastbone side of the meat.

STEP 2 FILLING POCKETS

Combine all ingredients for pesto filling in a blender or food processor. Hold open the pocket of one breast half and spoon in one quarter of the pesto mixture. Repeat with remaining breast halves and filling.

40

All you need to round out a meal of grilled chicken stuffed with pesto is an accompaniment of orzo pasta, perhaps studded with colourful diced peppers.

Surprise guests at your next barbecue with this succulent main course of citrus-soaked flattened chicken.

Butterflied Citrus Chicken

STEPS AT A GLANCE	Page
BUTTERFLYING WHOLE CHICKEN	43
MARINATING CHICKEN	92
BARBECUING CHICKEN	38

Preparation Time: 30 minutes
Marinating Time: 8 to 24 hours
Barbecuing Time: 60 to 70 minutes

INGREDIENTS

1	2-1/2- TO 3-LB/1.25- TO 1.5-KG ROASTING CHICKEN
3	FL OZ/80 ML OLIVE OIL *OR* COOKING OIL
3	FL OZ/80 ML ORANGE JUICE
2	FL OZ/60 ML LEMON JUICE
1-1/2	TEASPOONS DRIED ROSEMARY, CRUSHED
2	CLOVES GARLIC, MINCED
1/2	TEASPOON SALT
1/4	TEASPOON PEPPER

*B*utterflying chicken allows the maximum amount of surface area to be exposed to the barbecue. Use the indirect-heat method, as shown on page 39. The coals are medium hot when you can hold your hand above them for just 3 seconds.

■ Use poultry or kitchen shears to cut closely along both sides of the backbone for the entire length of chicken. Discard backbone. Turn skin-side up and open the bird out as flat as possible. Cover with clear plastic wrap. Strike breast firmly in the centre with the flat side of a meat mallet. (This breaks the breastbone so bird lies flat.) Twist wing tips under the back. Halfway between the legs and breastbone near the tip of the breast, cut a 1-in/2.5-cm slit through the skin on either side of and parallel with the breastbone. Insert drumstick tips into the slits. Place butterflied chicken in a large baking dish.

■ In a small mixing bowl stir together olive oil or cooking oil, orange juice, lemon juice, rosemary, garlic, salt, and pepper. Pour into a large plastic bag; add chicken. Seal bag; turn bag to coat chicken with marinade. Marinate in the refrigerator for 8 to 24 hours, turning bag occasionally. Drain marinade from chicken, reserving marinade.

■ In a covered barbecue arrange medium-hot coals on the grate around a drip pan, then test for medium heat above the pan. Place chicken, skin-side up, on the cooking rack directly over the drip pan, not over the coals. Brush with some of the reserved marinade. Cover and barbecue for 30 minutes. Brush with additional marinade. Cook for 30 to 40 minutes more, or till chicken is tender and no pink remains. Discard remaining marinade.

Makes 4 servings

Per serving: 332 calories, 31 g protein, 1 g carbohydrate, 22 g total fat (5 g saturated), 99 mg cholesterol, 163 mg sodium, 268 mg potassium

43

STEPS IN BUTTERFLYING WHOLE CHICKEN

STEP 1 REMOVING BACKBONE
Set the bird on the cutting board breast-side down. With kitchen scissors or poultry shears cut closely along one side of the backbone, then the other; discard backbone.

STEP 2 FLATTENING BIRD
Turn the chicken skin-side up with the breast facing you, wings up, legs down. Open the bird as flat as possible. Cover its surface with a large sheet of plastic wrap. Flatten by striking the breast firmly in the centre with the smooth side of a meat mallet to break the breastbone.

STEP 3 TUCKING LEGS INTO SLITS
Halfway between the legs and breastbone, near the bottom tip of the breast, cut a 1-in/2.5-cm slit through the loose skin on either side of and parallel with the breastbone. Insert the tips of the drumsticks into the slits to secure them so they won't pop up during barbecuing.

Japanese Chicken Kebabs

STEPS AT A GLANCE	Page
SKINNING & BONING CHICKEN	10
GRILLING CHICKEN	36

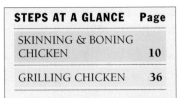

*S*erve these as a first course, too — warm or chilled. Allow 1 kebab per serving. When weather permits, cook the kebabs on the barbecue instead of under the grill. As a main course, serve the kebabs on a bed of fluffy steamed white rice.

■ Soak twelve 6-in/15-cm wooden skewers in water for 30 minutes. In a small mixing bowl combine the orange peel, orange juice, sherry, soy sauce, sugar, garlic, and ginger root. Set aside 2 fl oz/60 ml of the marinade mixture to serve with the cooked kebabs.

■ Cut chicken breast halves into 1-in/2.5-cm pieces. Cut green onions into 1½-in/4-cm lengths. Thread 3 chicken pieces and 2 onion pieces onto each wooden skewer, alternating chicken and onions. Place kebabs in a shallow dish and pour over marinade. Marinate at room temperature for 30 minutes, turning kebabs once. Remove kebabs from marinade, reserving marinade.

■ Preheat grill. Place kebabs on the unheated rack of a grill pan. Grill 4 in/10 cm from the heat for 8 to 10 minutes, or till chicken is tender and no pink remains, turning and brushing with reserved marinade once.

■ Meanwhile, heat the 2 fl oz/60 ml reserved marinade. Serve with kebabs, rice, and pickled ginger, if desired.

Makes 4 servings

Per serving: 251 calories, 20 g protein, 31 g carbohydrate, 3 g total fat (1 g saturated), 45 mg cholesterol, 960 mg sodium, 282 mg potassium

Preparation Time: 40 minutes
Marinating Time: 30 minutes
Grilling Time: 8 to 10 minutes

INGREDIENTS

1	TEASPOON FINELY SHREDDED ORANGE PEEL
4	FL OZ/125 ML ORANGE JUICE
3	FL OZ/90 ML DRY SHERRY
2	FL OZ/60 ML SOY SAUCE
2	TEASPOONS SUGAR
1	CLOVE GARLIC, MINCED
1/2	TEASPOON GRATED GINGERROOT
12	OZ/375 G BONELESS, SKINLESS CHICKEN BREAST HALVES
6	TO 8 SPRING ONIONS
	HOT COOKED RICE
	PICKLED GINGER (OPTIONAL)

Garnish this dish with Japanese flair by folding several slices of pickled ginger into a rose shape. To make spring onion spirals, thinly slice the tops lengthwise and float them in ice water until they curl.

44

Honey-glazed Drumsticks

A display of brightly coloured napkins and a bouquet of fresh herbs set off tantalising drumsticks.

STEPS AT A GLANCE	Page
GRILLING CHICKEN	36

Preparation Time: 15 minutes
Grilling Time: 25 to 30 minutes

INGREDIENTS

2	FL OZ/60 ML HONEY
2	TABLESPOONS SOY SAUCE
1	TABLESPOON CIDER VINEGAR
1	TABLESPOON MOLASSES *OR* GOLDEN SYRUP (OPTIONAL)
8	CHICKEN DRUMSTICKS (ABOUT 2-1/4 LB/1.125 KG TOTAL)

45

*T*hese *sweet, deliciously sticky drumsticks will encourage even the most polite diners to lick their fingers, so supply lots of napkins with this hands-on meal.*

■ In a small saucepan combine the honey, soy sauce, vinegar, and, if desired, molasses or golden syrup. Cook over medium-low heat for about 5 minutes, or till bubbly, stirring occasionally. (Watch mixture closely, as it will foam.)

■ Meanwhile, preheat grill. If desired, remove skin from chicken. Rinse chicken; pat dry. Place on a rack in an unheated grill pan. Grill 5 to 6 in/13 to 15 cm from the heat for about 15 minutes, or till chicken is light brown. Turn chicken and grill for 10 to 15 minutes more, or till chicken is tender and no pink remains. Brush chicken with glaze before the last 5 to 10 minutes of grilling. Before serving, spoon any remaining glaze over drumsticks.

Makes 4 servings

Per serving: 331 calories, 33 g protein, 18 g carbohydrate, 13 g total fat (4 g saturated), 111 mg cholesterol, 569 mg sodium, 307 mg potassium

Chicken Salad Niçoise

Preparation Time: 35 minutes
Marinating Time: 8 to 24 hours
Grilling Time: 12 to 16 minutes

INGREDIENTS

SALAD DRESSING

12	OZ/375 G BOTTLED *OR* TINNED MARINATED ARTICHOKE HEARTS
2	TABLESPOONS BALSAMIC VINEGAR
1	TABLESPOON DRAINED CAPERS
1	TABLESPOON ANCHOVY PASTE
1	TABLESPOON DIJON-STYLE MUSTARD
4	CLOVES GARLIC, MINCED
1/2	TEASPOON HERBES DE PROVENCE *OR* DRIED THYME LEAVES

SALAD

12	OZ/375 G BONELESS, SKINLESS CHICKEN BREAST HALVES
	SPINACH *OR* LETTUCE LEAVES
8	TINY NEW POTATOES, COOKED AND QUARTERED
2	MEDIUM TOMATOES, CUT INTO WEDGES
1	MEDIUM GREEN *AND/OR* RED PEPPER (CAPSICUM), CUT INTO STRIPS
2	HARD-BOILED EGGS, SLICED
1	FRESH FENNEL BULB, SLICED
1	OZ/30 G KALAMATA OLIVES *OR* PITTED RIPE OLIVES

Capture the sunny tastes of Provençal cuisine with this summer salad.

STEPS AT A GLANCE	Page
SKINNING & BONING CHICKEN	10
MARINATING CHICKEN	92
GRILLING CHICKEN	36

*T*his salad is a delicious twist on a French classic. We've used chicken instead of the customary tuna.

■ For salad dressing, drain artichokes, reserving liquid. In a screw-top jar combine the reserved artichoke liquid, vinegar, capers, anchovy paste, mustard, garlic, and herbes de Provence. Shake well.

■ For salad, in a large plastic bag combine chicken breast halves and 2 fl oz/60 ml of the salad dressing. (Cover and chill remaining salad dressing till serving time.) Seal bag and turn to coat chicken with dressing. Marinate in the refrigerator for 8 to 24 hours. Drain marinade from chicken; discard marinade.

■ Preheat grill. Place chicken on the unheated rack of a grill pan. Grill 5 to 6 in/13 to 15 cm from the heat for 6 to 8 minutes per side, or till tender and no pink remains. Cool slightly, then slice each chicken breast diagonally. Line a large serving platter with spinach or lettuce leaves. Arrange the chicken, artichokes, potatoes, tomatoes, pepper strips, eggs, fennel, and olives on platter. Drizzle all ingredients with remaining salad dressing just before serving.

Makes 4 servings

Per serving: 377 calories, 28 g protein, 39 g carbohydrate, 14 g total fat (2 g saturated), 155 mg cholesterol, 1,015 mg sodium, 1,337 mg potassium

Spicy Spanish Kebabs

STEPS AT A GLANCE	Page
SKINNING & BONING CHICKEN	10
MARINATING CHICKEN	92
BARBECUING CHICKEN	38

Preparation Time: 25 minutes
Marinating Time: 4 to 24 hours
Barbecuing Time: 10 to 12 minutes

INGREDIENTS

2	FL OZ/60 ML OLIVE OIL OR COOKING OIL
1	TABLESPOON LEMON JUICE
2	TABLESPOONS CHOPPED FRESH PARSLEY
1/2	TEASPOON GROUND CUMIN
1/4	TO 1/2 TEASPOON CRUSHED RED (CHILI) PEPPER FLAKES
1/2	TEASPOON DRIED THYME, CRUSHED
1/2	TEASPOON PAPRIKA
1/8	TEASPOON THREAD SAFFRON, CRUSHED
1/4	TEASPOON SALT
1/4	TEASPOON BLACK PEPPER
12	OZ/375 G BONELESS, SKINLESS CHICKEN THIGHS, CUT INTO 1-IN/2.5-CM CUBES OR 2X1-IN/ 5X2.5-CM STRIPS

*S*affron, the hand-gathered stigmas from a variety of Mediterranean crocus, is the most costly spice in the world. Ground turmeric can be used in its place; it will change the flavour of the dish only slightly.

■ In a medium mixing bowl stir together olive oil or cooking oil, lemon juice, parsley, cumin, red pepper, thyme, paprika, saffron, salt, and black pepper. Pour into a plastic bag; add chicken pieces. Seal bag; turn to coat chicken with marinade. Marinate in the refrigerator for 4 to 24 hours, turning the bag occasionally. Drain marinade from chicken, reserving marinade.

■ Thread chicken pieces on 4 long metal skewers, leaving about ¼ in/6 mm between pieces. Place chicken kebabs on the cooking rack of an uncovered barbecue. Barbecue directly over medium coals for 10 to 12 minutes, or till chicken is tender and no pink remains, turning once and brushing occasionally with reserved marinade.

Makes 4 servings

Per serving: 214 calories, 12 g protein, 1 g carbohydrate,
18 g total fat (3 g saturated), 41 mg cholesterol,
188 mg sodium, 136 mg potassium

A bed of golden rice, flavoured with saffron and peas, frames barbecued Spanish-style brochettes.

Firecracker Chicken Thighs

*A*vailable in Asian markets and some supermarkets, hot bean paste gives a tingling spiciness to this dish. To toast the sesame seeds, place them in a shallow pan and bake in a preheated 350°F/180°C oven for 7 to 10 minutes, or till golden.

■ Remove skin from chicken thighs. Score meat on both sides by making shallow diagonal cuts about 1 in/2.5 cm apart.

■ In a large mixing bowl stir together bean paste, soy sauce, sesame seeds, sesame oil, sugar, spring onions, garlic, salt, and pepper. Pour into a plastic bag; add chicken thighs. Seal bag; turn bag to coat chicken. Marinate in the refrigerator for 4 to 24 hours, turning bag occasionally. Remove chicken, scraping off excess marinade. Reserve marinade.

■ Place chicken on the cooking rack of an uncovered barbecue. Barbecue directly over medium coals for 15 minutes. Turn chicken over and barbecue for 10 to 15 minutes more. Baste both sides with reserved marinade and barbecue for 5 minutes more, or till chicken is tender and no pink remains, turning once. Discard any remaining marinade.

Makes 4 to 6 servings

Per serving: 359 calories, 22 g protein, 7 g carbohydrate, 28 g total fat (5 g saturated), 69 mg cholesterol, 525 mg sodium, 258 mg potassium

STEPS AT A GLANCE	Page
SKINNING CHICKEN THIGHS	10
SCORING & MARINATING CHICKEN	92
BARBECUING CHICKEN	38

Preparation Time: 20 minutes
Marinating Time: 4 to 24 hours
Barbecuing Time: 30 to 35 minutes

INGREDIENTS

1-1/2	TO 2 LB/750 G TO 1 KG CHICKEN THIGHS
2	TO 3 TABLESPOONS HOT BEAN PASTE
2	TABLESPOONS SOY SAUCE
2	TABLESPOONS TOASTED SESAME SEEDS, CRUSHED
1	TABLESPOON SESAME OIL
1	TABLESPOON SUGAR
1	OZ/30 G FINELY CHOPPED SPRING ONIONS
4	LARGE CLOVES GARLIC, MINCED (1 TABLESPOON)
1/4	TEASPOON SALT
1/8	TEASPOON PEPPER

48

Extend the Asian theme of this main course with grilled eggplant (aubergine) and steamed bok choy (or other greens) as accompaniments.

Frying & Sautéing

Steps in Pan-frying Chicken

BASIC TOOLS FOR PAN-FRYING

For pan-frying, use a pie plate and a plastic bag to hold the coatings and a heavy frying pan and tongs for cooking chicken.

LARGE FRYING PAN

PIE PLATE

TONGS

PLASTIC BAG

P AN-FRYING USES a small amount of fat, as opposed to deep-frying, which uses much more. Chicken cooked this way finishes juicy and flavourful, with a browned, crunchy exterior that is not at all greasy. To provide a barrier between the food and the cooking fat, pan-fried foods are usually coated in flour, then in a liquid such as milk, then again in either flour or bread crumbs, or just dipped in liquid and floured. These layers add texture, flavour, and colour.

Temperature control makes the difference between pan-fried chicken that is browned and chicken that is burnt or unevenly cooked. For the best results, select a frying pan with a heavy bottom that is responsive to changes in temperature, retains heat, and conducts it evenly. The pan should be large enough so you can cook a number of pieces in it at a time, with a handle that stays cool and is comfortable to hold. For safety, always turn the handle away from you so that you don't accidentally knock against it and spill the hot fat.

use a plastic bag to coat several chicken pieces at a time in the flour mixture

STEP 1 COATING CHICKEN PIECES

First dredge the chicken in flour so that the liquid has something to adhere to. Pour the buttermilk or other liquid into a pie plate and dip the flour-coated chicken in the buttermilk, then again in the flour mixture.

leave room between the pieces so that all sides of the chicken are exposed to the cooking oil

handle the pieces carefully when you turn them so that the coating stays intact

STEP 2 ADDING CHICKEN PIECES TO OIL

Add the oil to the frying pan and set the temperature to medium. When the fat is hot, place the coated chicken pieces in the pan with tongs and cook until the first side is evenly browned, about 15 minutes.

STEP 3 TURNING CHICKEN IN SKILLET

Once the pieces are nicely browned on one side, turn them to brown the other side. Reduce the heat to medium low and cook until the chicken is tender.

Succulent Crispy Fried Chicken (page 58) is the ultimate picnic food or the much-appreciated centrepiece of a family supper.

Steps in Sautéing Chicken

BASIC TOOLS FOR SAUTÉING CHICKEN

To successfully sauté chicken breasts, you need only these few simple tools: a roomy frying pan, a measuring cup, tongs, a wooden spoon, and a plate.

LARGE FRYING PAN

MEASURING CUP

SHALLOW PLATE

TONGS

WOODEN SPOON

52

COOKING FOODS quickly in a small amount of fat until nicely browned on the outside and tender and juicy within is the method known as sautéing. Most cuts of chicken with bones still in are sautéed only as a first step in braising (see page 86), but boneless chicken breasts or thighs are superb when cooked in this fashion and served with an easy-to-make pan sauce.

When a recipe calls for boneless, skinless chicken, see pages 10 and 11 to do your own boning and skinning, or buy the pieces already prepared. If desired, flatten each piece of chicken with a mallet as shown on page 20 to maximise the surface area and ensure even cooking. For a crisp crust that locks in moisture, dredge the chicken in seasoned flour before cooking (this step is not always necessary when sautéing). To finish, deglaze the pan with juice, broth, or wine, then stir in seasonings.

Once you are comfortable with sautéing, you can prepare an elegant party meal very quickly. It is ideal for impromptu dinners because it requires very little preparation, especially if your pantry is stocked with flour, seasonings, and deglazing liquids and your freezer has a supply of chicken breasts or thighs.

if the flour is unseasoned, sprinkle the chicken first with salt and pepper to flavour before dredging

STEP 1 COATING CHICKEN WITH FLOUR

Place flour on a plate. Hold the chicken (in this case, a boneless, skinless breast half) at one end and lay across the flour to coat. Lift the meat, turn, and place in the flour again to coat the other side.

turn the chicken with long-handled tongs so splatters don't burn your hand

stir with a wooden spoon, which won't get as hot as a metal utensil

STEP 2 SAUTÉING CHICKEN PIECES

Heat oil or butter in the pan. When the bubbles subside, add the chicken and cook until golden brown; turn and cook on the other side until it is evenly browned on the surface and opaque within. Transfer to a warm serving platter.

STEP 3 DEGLAZING PAN

Slowly pour the cold liquid into the hot pan to dislodge the browned bits left on the bottom when the chicken was browned. Stir and boil to concentrate the flavours of the sauce.

To serve, return the cooked chicken to the pan with the sauce to reheat it quickly, then transfer to a plate and drizzle with the sauce. The recipe for this classic dish, Sherried Chicken with Orange Sauce, appears on page 64.

53

reducing the liquid thickens the sauce and intensifies its flavour

STEP 4 THICKENING SAUCE

Let the sauce cook until some of the liquid is evaporated and the volume is reduced to about half the original amount. Taste before serving and adjust the seasonings, if necessary.

Sautéed Breasts with Beurre Blanc

STEPS AT A GLANCE	Page
SKINNING & BONING CHICKEN	10
SAUTÉING CHICKEN	52
MAKING BEURRE BLANC	54

54

*B*eurre blanc, a renowned French sauce, breaks down easily and cannot be reheated. If it turns oily, beat a spoonful of it in a chilled bowl until creamy, then add the rest of the sauce a spoonful at a time.

■ Rinse chicken; pat dry. In a large frying pan heat oil over medium heat. Add chicken and cook for 10 to 12 minutes, or till tender and no pink remains, turning once. Sprinkle chicken with salt and pepper.

■ Meanwhile, in a heavy small saucepan combine shallots or spring onions, vinegar, and dry sherry. Bring to boiling; boil, uncovered, for about 4 minutes, or till about 1 tablespoon of liquid remains. With a wire whisk, whisk in cream and boil gently for 2 to 3 minutes, or till thickened. Remove pan from heat. Whisk in butter 1 piece at a time, allowing butter to melt completely before adding the next piece of butter. Season to taste with white pepper. If desired, strain the sauce to remove chopped shallots. Serve immediately over chicken.

Makes 4 servings

Per serving: 339 calories, 22 g protein, 3 g carbohydrate, 25 g total fat (13 g saturated), 111 mg cholesterol, 297 mg sodium, 211 mg potassium

Preparation Time: 15 minutes
Cooking Time: 10 to 12 minutes

INGREDIENTS

4	BONELESS, SKINLESS CHICKEN BREAST HALVES (1 LB/500 G TOTAL)
1	TABLESPOON OLIVE OIL *OR* COOKING OIL
	SALT
	PEPPER
2	TABLESPOONS FINELY CHOPPED SHALLOTS *OR* SPRING ONIONS
2	FL OZ/60 ML SHERRY WINE VINEGAR *OR* WHITE WINE VINEGAR
2	FL OZ/60 ML DRY SHERRY
1	TABLESPOON HEAVY (DOUBLE) CREAM
3	OZ/90 G BUTTER (AT ROOM TEMPERATURE), CUT INTO 6 PIECES
1/8	TEASPOON WHITE PEPPER

STEPS IN MAKING BEURRE BLANC

STEP 1 **ADDING BUTTER**
After boiling down the shallot mixture and adding the whipping cream, boil the sauce gently for 2 to 3 minutes to thicken. Remove from the heat and whisk in the first piece of butter. Incorporate each piece of butter completely before adding the next.

STEP 2 **FINISHING SAUCE**
As the butter is blended into the sauce mixture, the sauce becomes silky and smooth. Remember to incorporate each piece of butter completely before adding the next; this keeps the sauce at the right consistency. Season with pepper, strain to remove the shallots, then spoon over the chicken.

Create a culinary masterpiece featuring
chicken in a rich butter sauce, sautéed
vegetables, and roasted sliced potatoes.

This ratatouille-like dish is ideal on a warm summer's eve. All it needs is some crusty bread and a crisp salad drizzled with vinaigrette.

Chicken Provençale

INGREDIENTS

10	OZ/300 G CUBED PEELED EGG-PLANT (AUBERGINE)
2	MEDIUM TOMATOES, PEELED, SEEDED, AND CHOPPED
1	MEDIUM ONION, HALVED AND THINLY SLICED
1	MEDIUM RED PEPPER (CAPSICUM), CUT INTO THIN STRIPS
1	MEDIUM GREEN PEPPER (CAPSICUM), CUT INTO THIN STRIPS
2	FL OZ/60 ML RED OR DRY WHITE WINE, *OR* CHICKEN STOCK
2	TABLESPOONS CHOPPED FRESH BASIL *OR* 1-1/2 TEASPOONS DRIED BASIL, CRUSHED
2	CLOVES GARLIC, MINCED
1/2	TEASPOON SALT
4	BONELESS, SKINLESS CHICKEN BREAST HALVES (1 LB/500 G TOTAL)
	SALT
1	TABLESPOON OLIVE OIL *OR* COOKING OIL
1/2	TEASPOON PAPRIKA

*F*or a naturally light main dish, these chicken breasts are served with an earthy vegetable stew. The meat is cooked in minimal oil and the vegetables are steamed in wine.

■ In a large saucepan combine the eggplant (aubergine), tomatoes, onion, red and green peppers, wine or chicken stock, basil, garlic, and ½ teaspoon salt. Bring to boiling; reduce heat. Simmer, covered, for 10 minutes. Uncover and simmer for 5 minutes more, or till vegetables are tender and nearly all of the liquid is evaporated.

■ Meanwhile, rinse chicken; pat dry. Place each breast half between 2 pieces of plastic wrap. Working from the centre to the edges, pound chicken lightly with the flat side of a meat mallet to a ¼-in/6-mm thickness. Remove plastic wrap. Sprinkle chicken lightly with salt.

■ In a large frying pan heat the oil and paprika over medium-high heat. Add the chicken and cook for 4 to 6 minutes, or till tender and no pink remains, turning once. To serve, spoon vegetables on plates and top with chicken.

Makes 4 servings

Per serving: 209 calories, 23 g protein, 11 g carbohydrate, 7 g total fat (1 g saturated), 59 mg cholesterol, 370 mg sodium, 552 mg potassium

Preparation Time: 30 minutes
Cooking Time: 19 to 21 minutes

STEPS AT A GLANCE	Page
PREPARING TOMATOES & HERBS	57
SKINNING & BONING CHICKEN	10
POUNDING CHICKEN BREASTS	20
SAUTÉING CHICKEN	52

STEPS IN PREPARING TOMATOES AND HERBS

STEP 1 PEELING TOMATOES
Make an X at the blossom end (bottom) of the tomato. Plunge the tomato into boiling water for 30 seconds; remove and cool in ice water, then drain. To peel, pull back one segment of skin at the X. Repeat with remaining skin.

STEP 2 SEEDING TOMATOES
After peeling, cut the tomato in half crosswise between the stem and blossom ends. Holding it upside down, gently squeeze each half to push out the seeds from the cavities. If some seeds remain, pick them out with a paring knife, grapefruit spoon, or your fingers.

STEP 3 CHOPPING FRESH BASIL
Put the basil leaves in a small measuring cup or ramekin. If the leaves are large, stack them first and cut them into pieces. With kitchen scissors, chop them to the appropriate size.

Crispy Fried Chicken

STEPS AT A GLANCE	Page
PAN-FRYING CHICKEN	50

Preparation Time: 15 minutes
Cooking Time: 50 to 55 minutes

INGREDIENTS

CHICKEN

4	OZ/125 G PLAIN FLOUR
1-1/2	TEASPOONS DRIED BASIL, CRUSHED
1/2	TEASPOON SALT
1/2	TEASPOON ONION POWDER
1/4	TEASPOON PEPPER
1	3- TO 3-1/2-LB/1.5- TO 1.75-KG ROASTING CHICKEN, CUT UP
4	FL OZ/125 ML BUTTERMILK
2	TABLESPOONS COOKING OIL

GRAVY

2	TABLESPOONS PLAIN FLOUR
1	TEASPOON INSTANT CHICKEN STOCK GRANULES *OR* CONCENTRATE
1/8	TEASPOON PEPPER
14	FL OZ/430 ML MILK

*E*njoy this tried-and-true favourite warm with gravy for a family dinner or chilled and plain for your next picnic. If making the chicken ahead of time, be sure to refrigerate it until it's cold and transport it in an iced container.

■ For chicken, in a plastic bag combine flour, basil, salt, onion powder, and pepper. Set aside. If desired, remove skin from chicken. Rinse chicken; pat dry. Add chicken pieces 2 or 3 at a time to plastic bag, shaking bag to coat chicken pieces with flour mixture. Dip pieces, one at a time, into buttermilk. Add again to plastic bag with flour mixture, shaking to coat well.

■ In a 12-in/30-cm frying pan cook the chicken in hot oil for 15 minutes over medium heat, turning to brown evenly. Reduce heat to medium-low and cook, uncovered, for 35 to 40 minutes more, or till chicken is tender and no pink remains, turning occasionally. Remove chicken from frying pan; drain on paper towels. Transfer chicken to a serving platter; keep warm while making gravy.

■ For gravy, stir flour, stock granules, and pepper into drippings in frying pan, scraping up browned bits. Add milk all at once. Cook and stir over medium heat till thickened and bubbly. Cook and stir for 1 minute more. Serve gravy with chicken.

Makes 6 servings

Per serving: 380 calories, 30 g protein, 21 g carbohydrate, 19 g fat (5 g saturated), 85 mg cholesterol, 453 mg sodium, 382 mg potassium

What could be better with fried chicken and gravy than a warm bread roll and butter? Some sliced tomatoes would be nice on a summer menu, or hot vegetables in the winter.

58

Tangy Marinated Fried Chicken

Oven-roasted new potatoes and
steamed broccoli flank fried
chicken for a simple dinner
at any time of year.

Preparation Time: 15 minutes
Marinating Time: 8 to 24 hours
Cooking Time: 40 to 50 minutes

INGREDIENTS

MARINADE

4	CLOVES GARLIC
1/2	TEASPOON SALT
3	FL OZ/90 ML LIME JUICE
2	TABLESPOONS OLIVE OIL *OR* COOKING OIL
2	TABLESPOONS WATER
1	TEASPOON GROUND CUMIN
1/4	TEASPOON GROUND TURMERIC
1/4	TEASPOON PEPPER

FRIED CHICKEN

2	TO 2-1/2 LB/1 TO 1.25 KG MEATY CHICKEN PIECES (BREASTS, THIGHS, AND DRUMSTICKS)
1	OZ/30 G PLAIN FLOUR
2	TABLESPOONS OLIVE OIL *OR* COOKING OIL

*R*esist the temptation to save a few calories and
leave the skin on this chicken. It crisps up nicely
and turns a beautiful brown for a lovely appearance.

■ For marinade, use a mortar and pestle or a bowl and wooden
spoon to mash the garlic with the salt until a paste is formed. In a
small bowl combine the garlic-salt mixture, lime juice, 2 tablespoons
olive oil or cooking oil, water, cumin, turmeric, and pepper.

■ For fried chicken, rinse chicken; pat dry. Pour marinade into a plastic bag; add chicken
pieces. Seal bag; turn bag to coat chicken with marinade. Marinate in the refrigerator for
8 to 24 hours, turning bag occasionally. Drain marinade from chicken; discard marinade.
Pat chicken dry with paper towels.

■ Place flour in a clean plastic bag. Add chicken, 2 or 3 pieces at a time; shake bag to coat
chicken with flour. In a large ovenproof pan heat 2 tablespoons olive oil or cooking oil.
Add chicken and cook, uncovered, over medium-low heat for 10 to 15 minutes, turning
to brown evenly. Spoon off fat. Transfer pan to a preheated 375°F/190°C oven. Bake,
uncovered, for 30 to 35 minutes, or till chicken is tender and no pink remains.

Makes 4 servings

Per serving: 366 calories, 34 g protein, 6 g carbohydrate, 22 g total fat (5 g saturated), 104 mg cholesterol, 188 mg sodium,
269 mg potassium

STEPS AT A GLANCE	Page
MARINATING CHICKEN	92
PAN-FRYING CHICKEN	50

59

Sautéed Chicken with Fresh Tomato Chutney

STEPS AT A GLANCE	Page
SAUTÉING CHICKEN	52

Preparation Time: 30 minutes
Cooking Time: 40 to 45 minutes

INGREDIENTS

2	LB/1 KG CHICKEN THIGHS, SKINNED, IF DESIRED
1	TABLESPOON COOKING OIL
2	MEDIUM TOMATOES, PEELED, SEEDED, AND CHOPPED
2	TART COOKING APPLES, CHOPPED
1	SMALL HOT CHILI, SEEDED AND FINELY CHOPPED
1-1/2	OZ/45 G CURRANTS OR RAISINS
2-1/2	OZ/75 G CHOPPED RED PEPPER (CAPSICUM)
2	OZ/60 G CHOPPED ONION
2	FL OZ/60 ML CIDER VINEGAR
1	TABLESPOON SUGAR
2	TEASPOONS GRATED GINGER ROOT
1/4	TEASPOON SALT

*C*hutney *is a general term used for any number of pickled fruit or vegetable combinations. Usually chutneys are highly spiced, like this instant version.*

The chutney served with this chicken is so chunky and fresh, it plays the role of a vegetable. Complete the meal with a starch, such as mashed potatoes.

■ Rinse chicken; pat dry. In a large frying pan heat cooking oil over medium-high heat. Add chicken thighs and brown quickly on both sides. Spoon off fat.

■ In a large mixing bowl stir together tomatoes, apples, chili, currants or raisins, red pepper, onion, vinegar, sugar, ginger root, and salt. Add to the frying pan with the chicken. Bring to boiling; reduce heat. Cover and simmer for about 35 to 40 minutes, or till chicken is tender and no pink remains. Remove chicken from frying pan; keep warm. Boil tomato-apple mixture, uncovered, for about 5 minutes, or till thickened. Serve with chicken.

Makes 4 servings

Per serving: 334 calories, 24 g protein, 27 g carbohydrate, 15 g total fat (4 g saturated), 77 mg cholesterol, 229 mg sodium, 642 mg potassium

Coconut Chicken

*C*oconut milk gives this dish a creamy consistency and a mild but distinct flavour unlike that of coconut in its many sweetened incarnations. For more information on coconut milk and where to buy it, see the glossary on page 118.

■ In a large frying pan brown the chicken drumsticks in hot oil for about 8 minutes, turning to brown evenly. Remove chicken from frying pan and set aside.

■ In the same frying pan cook the onion for 5 minutes, or till tender but not brown. Stir in the curry powder and cook for 1 minute. Stir in the lemon peel, lemon juice, and salt. Carefully stir in the coconut milk. Bring mixture to boiling; return chicken to frying pan. Reduce heat and simmer, covered, for 30 to 40 minutes, or till chicken is tender and no pink remains, turning chicken once and stirring occasionally. Serve chicken sprinkled with toasted coconut.

Makes 4 servings

Per serving: 619 calories, 31 g protein, 35 g carbohydrate, 39 g total fat (19 g saturated), 90 mg cholesterol, 250 mg sodium, 599 mg potassium

INGREDIENTS

8	CHICKEN DRUMSTICKS (2 LB/1 KG TOTAL)
2	TABLESPOONS COOKING OIL
1	MEDIUM ONION, HALVED AND THINLY SLICED
1	TEASPOON CURRY POWDER
1	TEASPOON FINELY SHREDDED LEMON PEEL
1	TABLESPOON LEMON JUICE
1/4	TEASPOON SALT
10	FL OZ/310 ML TINNED COCONUT MILK (UNSWEETENED)
1	OZ/30 G TOASTED DESICCATED COCONUT

Preparation Time: 20 minutes
Cooking Time: 44 to 54 minutes

STEPS AT A GLANCE	Page
SAUTÉING CHICKEN	52

Coated in a luscious coconut sauce, these drumsticks are irresistible on a bed of julienned vegetables, such as carrots, zucchini (courgettes), and red peppers.

Chicken Legs with Beer Barbecue Sauce

Preparation Time: 15 minutes
Cooking Time: 42 to 53 minutes

STEPS AT A GLANCE	Page
SAUTÉING CHICKEN	52

INGREDIENTS

2	LB/1 KG CHICKEN DRUMSTICKS *AND/OR* THIGHS, SKINNED, IF DESIRED
1	TABLESPOON COOKING OIL
1	OZ/30 G CHOPPED ONION
8	FL OZ/250 ML SWEET CHILI SAUCE
4	FL OZ/125 ML BEER
2	TABLESPOONS BROWN SUGAR
1/2	TEASPOON GROUND CUMIN
1/2	TEASPOON PREPARED MUSTARD
1/8	TEASPOON PEPPER
	FEW DROPS HOT CHILI SAUCE

*E*njoy the flavour of barbecued chicken without lighting the barbecue! Just sauté chicken pieces instead, then simmer them in a piquant sauce.

■ Rinse chicken; pat dry. In a large frying pan heat oil. Add chicken and cook, uncovered, over medium heat for 10 to 15 minutes, turning to brown evenly. Drain off fat. Add the onion to chicken and cook for 2 to 3 minutes.

■ In a small mixing bowl combine the sweet chili sauce, beer, brown sugar, cumin, mustard, pepper, and hot chili sauce. Pour the sauce over the chicken. Bring to boiling; reduce heat. Simmer, covered, for 20 minutes. Uncover and turn chicken. Simmer, uncovered, for 10 to 15 minutes more, or till chicken is tender and no pink remains. Transfer chicken to a serving platter; keep warm.

■ Skim excess fat off sauce in frying pan. Simmer sauce, uncovered, to desired consistency. Serve sauce with meat.

Makes 4 servings

Per serving: 384 calories, 31 g protein, 24 g carbohydrate, 17 g total fat (4 g saturated), 103 mg cholesterol, 915 mg sodium, 530 mg potassium

Whole ears of fresh corn are a natural complement to chicken simmered in a spicy sauce.

Chicken Fajitas

STEPS AT A GLANCE	Page
MARINATING CHICKEN	92
SAUTÉING CHICKEN	52

Preparation Time: 30 minutes
Marinating Time: 4 to 24 hours
Cooking Time: 6 to 8 minutes

INGREDIENTS

12	OZ/375 G BONELESS, SKINLESS CHICKEN BREAST HALVES, CUT INTO 2-IN X 1/2-IN/5-CM X 12-MM STRIPS
2	FL OZ/60 ML COOKING OIL
2	FL OZ/60 ML FRESH LIME JUICE
2	FL OZ/60 ML TEQUILA *OR* WATER
2	TABLESPOONS CHOPPED FRESH CORIANDER (CHINESE PARSLEY)
2	CLOVES GARLIC, MINCED
1	TEASPOON GROUND CUMIN
1/8	TEASPOON SALT
	PEPPER
8	7-IN/18-CM FLOUR TORTILLAS
1	TABLESPOON COOKING OIL
1	MEDIUM ONION, HALVED AND THINLY SLICED
1	MEDIUM GREEN, RED, *OR* YELLOW PEPPER (CAPSICUM), CUT INTO THIN STRIPS
3	OZ/90 G CHOPPED FRESH *OR* TINNED TOMATILLOS, *OR* CHOPPED TOMATOES
	GUACAMOLE (OPTIONAL)
	SOUR CREAM (OPTIONAL)
	SALSA (OPTIONAL)
	SHREDDED CHEDDAR CHEESE (OPTIONAL)

*M*exican fajitas have become the rage in restaurants in recent years. They are parcels of meat or chicken and vegetables wrapped in tortillas. If you can't get tortillas, the chicken and peppers are good on a bed of rice. Use tomatoes instead of tomatillos for more colour.

■ Place chicken strips in a plastic bag set in a deep bowl. In another bowl stir together 2 fl oz/ 60 ml oil, lime juice, tequila or water, 1 tablespoon of the coriander, the garlic, cumin, salt, and pepper. Pour over chicken. Seal bag and marinate in the refrigerator for 4 to 24 hours, turning occasionally. Drain chicken; discard marinade. Set chicken aside.

■ Wrap tortillas in foil. Heat in a 350°F/180°C oven for 10 minutes to warm. Meanwhile, pre-heat a large frying pan over medium-high heat; add 1 tablespoon oil. Cook and stir onion in hot oil for 1½ minutes. Add pepper strips; cook and stir about 1½ minutes more, or till vegetables are crisp-tender. Remove vegetables from frying pan.

■ Add chicken strips to hot frying pan. (Add more oil, if necessary.) Cook and stir for 2 to 3 minutes, or till tender and no pink remains. Return all vegetables to frying pan. Add tomatillos or tomatoes. Cook and stir for 1 to 2 minutes, or till heated through. Stir in remaining coriander. To serve, fill tortillas with chicken-vegetable mixture. If desired, top with guacamole, sour cream, salsa, and/or cheese.

Makes 4 servings

Per serving: 497 calories, 22 g protein, 42 g carbohydrate,
23 g total fat (4 g saturated), 45 mg cholesterol,
341 mg sodium, 375 mg potassium

Chicken strips, sautéed with peppers and onions, are rolled into a tortilla and served with assorted toppings for an all-in-one meal.

Sherried Chicken with Orange Sauce

For a smart dinner party, present these
sherry-laced chicken breasts on
parsleyed rice with peas and
bread rolls.

64

Preparation Time: 15 minutes
Cooking Time: 13 to 17 minutes

INGREDIENTS

4	BONELESS, SKINLESS CHICKEN BREAST HALVES (1 LB/500 G TOTAL)
1	OZ/30 G PLAIN FLOUR
1/2	TEASPOON SALT
1/4	TEASPOON PEPPER
2	TABLESPOONS OLIVE OIL OR COOKING OIL
1	CLOVE GARLIC, CUT INTO THIN SLIVERS
4	FL OZ/125 ML CREAM SHERRY
8	FL OZ/250 ML ORANGE JUICE
2	TABLESPOONS ORANGE MARMALADE
1	OZ/30 G FLAKED ALMONDS, TOASTED
	HOT COOKED RICE

*A*nother time, try serving this chicken and its
*citrus sauce over plain or saffron-flavoured
fresh pasta, available at gourmet food shops.*

STEPS AT A GLANCE	Page
SKINNING & BONING CHICKEN	10
SAUTÉING CHICKEN	52

■ Rinse chicken; pat dry. In a large plastic bag combine flour, salt, and pepper. Add chicken, 1 piece at a time, shaking bag to coat chicken with flour mixture. In a 10-in/25-cm frying pan heat olive oil or cooking oil over medium heat. Add chicken and cook for 10 to 12 minutes, or till chicken is tender and no longer pink, turning once. Transfer chicken to a serving platter; keep warm.

■ In the same frying pan cook and stir garlic in the pan drippings for 15 seconds. Carefully add cream sherry. Bring to boiling; boil gently, uncovered, for 1 to 2 minutes, or till reduced by half. Stir in orange juice and orange marmalade. Bring to boiling; boil gently, uncovered, for 2 to 3 minutes, or till slightly thickened. Pour over chicken. Sprinkle with toasted almonds. Serve with rice.

Makes 4 servings

Per serving: 472 calories, 27 g protein, 50 g carbohydrate, 15 g total fat (2 g saturated), 59 mg cholesterol, 327 mg sodium, 432 mg potassium

Chicken Diana

*I*f you want to make an impression on your dinner guests, invite them into the kitchen for the flaming, which makes a good show but also serves to burn off the alcohol and leave the brandy flavour.

■ Rinse chicken; pat dry. Place each breast half between 2 pieces of plastic wrap. Working from the centre to the edges, pound chicken lightly with the flat side of a meat mallet to a ¼-in/6-mm thickness. Remove plastic wrap.

■ In a 12-in/30-cm frying pan melt margarine or butter. Add shallots and cook over medium heat till tender. Increase heat to medium-high. Add chicken and cook for 4 to 6 minutes, or till chicken is tender and no pink remains, turning once. Remove from heat. Sprinkle chicken with brandy. Ignite the brandy using a very long match while keeping your hand to the side of the frying pan. When flame is gone, transfer chicken to a serving platter and keep warm.

■ In a small mixing bowl stir together chicken stock, Worcestershire sauce, and mustard; add to frying pan. Bring to boiling; boil gently about 5 minutes to slightly thicken liquid and reduce it by half. Pour sauce over chicken breasts. Sprinkle with parsley.

Makes 4 servings

Per serving: 204 calories, 23 g protein, 3 g carbohydrate, 9 g total fat
(2 g saturated), 60 mg cholesterol, 313 mg sodium, 251 mg potassium

Preparation Time: 15 minutes
Cooking Time: 10 to 12 minutes

INGREDIENTS

4	BONELESS, SKINLESS CHICKEN BREAST HALVES (1 LB/500 G TOTAL)
2	TABLESPOONS MARGARINE OR BUTTER
2	SHALLOTS, FINELY CHOPPED
2	TABLESPOONS BRANDY
4	FL OZ/125 ML CHICKEN STOCK
2	TABLESPOONS WHITE WINE WORCESTERSHIRE SAUCE *OR* PLAIN WORCESTERSHIRE SAUCE
1	TEASPOON DIJON-STYLE MUSTARD
2	TABLESPOONS CHOPPED FRESH PARSLEY

STEPS AT A GLANCE	Page
SKINNING & BONING CHICKEN	10
POUNDING CHICKEN BREASTS	20
SAUTÉING CHICKEN	52

65

An impressive main course, Chicken Diana merits equally lovely accompaniments. Wide egg noodles with poppy seeds, and asparagus spears strewn with red pepper are perfect choices.

Chicken Piccata with Vegetables

*R*ich fettuccine Alfredo, or just buttered pasta, would be delightful with this lemon-flavoured main course. Garnish with lemon and parsley.

■ Rinse chicken; pat dry. Place each breast half between 2 pieces of plastic wrap. Working from the centre to the edges, pound chicken lightly with the flat side of a meat mallet to a ¼-in/6-mm thickness. Remove plastic wrap.

■ In a shallow dish stir together the flour, salt, and pepper. Coat each breast with flour mixture; shake off excess.

■ In a 12-in/30-cm skillet melt half the margarine or butter. Add chicken and cook over medium-high heat for 4 to 6 minutes, or till tender and no pink remains, turning once. Remove chicken from frying pan; keep warm. In the same pan combine the chicken stock, wine, lemon peel, and lemon juice. Bring to boiling; boil till sauce is reduced to about 3 fl oz/80 ml. Remove from heat and stir in parsley.

■ Meanwhile, in a 10-in/25-cm frying pan melt the remaining margarine or butter. Add the carrots, zucchini, and garlic and cook for 2 to 3 minutes, or till carrots are crisp-tender. Transfer vegetables to a platter, top with chicken and sauce.

Makes 4 servings

Per serving: 267 calories, 24 g protein, 13 g carbohydrate, 12 g total fat (3 g saturated), 60 mg cholesterol, 296 mg sodium, 487 mg potassium

Preparation Time: 25 minutes
Cooking Time: 6 to 8 minutes

STEPS AT A GLANCE	Page
SKINNING & BONING CHICKEN	10
POUNDING CHICKEN BREASTS	20
SAUTÉING CHICKEN	52

INGREDIENTS

4	BONELESS, SKINLESS CHICKEN BREAST HALVES (1 LB/500 G TOTAL)
1	OZ/30 G PLAIN FLOUR
1/8	TEASPOON SALT
1/8	TEASPOON PEPPER
3	TABLESPOONS MARGARINE *OR* BUTTER
2	FL OZ/60 ML CHICKEN STOCK
2	FL OZ/60 ML DRY WHITE WINE, DRY WHITE VERMOUTH, *OR* CHICKEN STOCK
1	TABLESPOON FINELY SHREDDED LEMON PEEL
2	TABLESPOONS LEMON JUICE
2	TABLESPOONS CHOPPED FRESH PARSLEY
2	MEDIUM CARROTS, SHREDDED
2	MEDIUM ZUCCHINI, SHREDDED
1	CLOVE GARLIC, MINCED

A modern version of an Italian classic made with veal, this chicken-based piccata features the characteristic tart sauce plus a crunchy layer of sautéed vegetables.

66

Chicken with Duxelles Wrapped in Phyllo

Preparation Time: 25 minutes
Cooking Time: 12 to 13 minutes
Baking Time: 25 minutes

Coat a sautéed chicken breast with duxelles, then wrap in phyllo for a stylish light meal.

INGREDIENTS

1	TABLESPOON COOKING OIL
4	SKINLESS, BONELESS CHICKEN BREAST HALVES (1 LB/500 G TOTAL)
1	TABLESPOON MARGARINE OR BUTTER
8	OZ/250 G FRESH MUSHROOMS, FINELY CHOPPED
2	SPRING ONIONS, FINELY CHOPPED
1	TABLESPOON DRY WHITE VERMOUTH OR DRY WHITE WINE (OPTIONAL)
1/4	TEASPOON SALT
1/4	TEASPOON DRIED THYME, CRUSHED
	DASH PEPPER
2	TABLESPOONS SOUR CREAM
8	SHEETS PHYLLO DOUGH, THAWED
6	TABLESPOONS MARGARINE OR BUTTER, MELTED

67

*T*he culinary term duxelles *refers to a cooked mixture of mushrooms and onions. The finished duxelles may be frozen for several weeks. When working with phyllo, keep the extra sheets covered with a damp towel so they don't dry out.*

■ In a large frying pan heat oil and brown the chicken breasts on both sides. Remove and set aside. In the same skillet melt the margarine or butter over medium-high heat. Add mushrooms and onions; cook and stir for about 5 minutes, or till most of the liquid evaporates. Stir in vermouth (if desired), salt, thyme, and pepper. Cook for 2 to 3 minutes more, or till all the liquid has evaporated. Let cool, then stir in sour cream.

■ Brush 1 sheet of phyllo with some of the melted margarine or butter. Place another sheet of phyllo on the first sheet and brush with margarine or butter. (Keep remaining phyllo covered with a damp towel.) Place a chicken breast in the centre of one short end. Spread the top of the chicken with about a quarter of the mushroom mixture. Fold both long sides of phyllo toward the centre and brush with margarine or butter. Roll up. Place on a baking sheet and brush top and sides with margarine or butter. Repeat with remaining phyllo, mushroom mixture, chicken breasts, and margarine or butter.

■ Bake in a preheated 375°F/190°C oven for about 25 minutes, or till phyllo is golden and chicken is tender and no pink remains.

Makes 4 servings

Per serving: 440 calories, 26 g protein, 22 g carbohydrate, 28 g total fat (6 g saturated), 62 mg cholesterol, 531 mg sodium, 422 mg potassium

STEPS AT A GLANCE	Page
SKINNING & BONING CHICKEN	10
SAUTÉING CHICKEN	52

Chicken Breasts with Sauce Suprême

STEPS AT A GLANCE	Page
SKINNING & BONING CHICKEN	10
SAUTÉING CHICKEN	52

Preparation Time: 20 minutes
Cooking Time: 15 to 17 minutes

INGREDIENTS

2	TABLESPOONS MARGARINE *OR* BUTTER
4	BONELESS, SKINLESS CHICKEN BREAST HALVES (1 LB/500 G TOTAL)
	SALT
	PEPPER
1-1/2	OZ/45 G SLICED FRESH MUSHROOMS
1	OZ/30 G FINELY CHOPPED SHALLOTS
2	FL OZ/60 ML DRY WHITE WINE
8	FL OZ/250 ML CHICKEN STOCK
2	TABLESPOONS PLAIN FLOUR
2	TEASPOONS CHOPPED FRESH THYME *OR* 1/2 TEASPOON DRIED THYME, CRUSHED
1	BAY LEAF
3	TABLESPOONS HEAVY (DOUBLE) CREAM
	SALT
	WHITE PEPPER
	HOT COOKED LINGUINE *OR* FETTUCCINE

68

*T*his elegant dish is surprisingly simple to make. Have everything prepared and measured in advance so you can work quickly, and keep a wooden spoon handy to blend in all the tasty bits in the drippings.

■ In a large frying pan melt margarine or butter over medium heat. Add chicken breasts and cook for 10 to 12 minutes, or till chicken is tender and no pink remains, turning once. Sprinkle chicken with salt and pepper. Transfer to a serving platter; keep warm.

■ In the same frying pan cook mushrooms and shallots in the chicken drippings for about 3 minutes, or till tender. Spoon over chicken; keep warm. Add white wine to pan, stirring to loosen crusty browned bits in the bottom of the pan. Stir together chicken stock, flour, thyme, and bay leaf. Add to pan. Cook and stir till thickened and bubbly. Cook for 2 minutes more. Stir in cream. Remove bay leaf. Season sauce to taste with salt and white pepper. Serve sauce over chicken and hot cooked pasta.

Makes 4 servings

Per serving: 353 calories, 28 g protein, 28 g carbohydrate, 14 g total fat (5 g saturated), 75 mg cholesterol, 420 mg sodium, 332 mg potassium

Serve these golden chicken breasts on pasta and circle with steamed julienned zucchini (courgettes) and carrots.

Sautéed Chicken Sandwich with Olives

STEPS AT A GLANCE	Page
SKINNING & BONING CHICKEN	10
POUNDING CHICKEN BREASTS	20
SAUTÉING CHICKEN	52

Preparation Time: 20 minutes
Cooking Time: 4 to 6 minutes

INGREDIENTS

1-1/2	OZ/45 G CHOPPED PIMIENTO-STUFFED OLIVES OR KALAMATA OLIVES
1	SMALL TOMATO, CHOPPED
1	TABLESPOON CHOPPED FRESH PARSLEY
2	TEASPOONS DRAINED CAPERS (OPTIONAL)
1/2	TEASPOON DRIED ITALIAN SEASONING, CRUSHED
1	TEASPOON OLIVE OIL OR COOKING OIL
4	BONELESS, SKINLESS CHICKEN BREAST HALVES (1 LB/500 G TOTAL)
2	TABLESPOONS OLIVE OIL OR COOKING OIL
4	LETTUCE LEAVES
4	SLICES SOURDOUGH BREAD, TOASTED

69

*T*urn *this recipe into delicious party snacks by leaving out the chicken and simply spreading the olive mixture on slices of sourdough bread that have been brushed with olive oil and toasted under the grill.*

■ In a small mixing bowl stir together olives, tomato, parsley, capers (if desired), Italian seasoning, and the 1 teaspoon olive oil or cooking oil. Set aside.

■ Place each breast half between 2 pieces of plastic wrap. Working from the centre to the edges, pound chicken lightly with the flat side of a meat mallet to a ¼-in/6-mm thickness. Remove plastic wrap.

■ In a large frying pan cook chicken in the 2 tablespoons olive oil or cooking oil over medium-high heat for 4 to 6 minutes, or till tender and no pink remains, turning once. Remove from frying pan. To serve, place lettuce leaves on toasted sourdough bread. Top with chicken breasts and olive mixture.

Makes 4 servings

Per serving: 226 calories, 25 g protein, 18 g carbohydrate, 5 g total fat (1 g saturated), 50 mg cholesterol, 387 mg sodium, 261 mg potassium

Plan a bistro-style menu with these sautéed chicken breast sandwiches accompanied by thin French fries, or *pommes frites*.

Rhineland Chicken Burgers

STEPS AT A GLANCE	Page
SAUTÉING CHICKEN PIECES	53

Preparation Time: 15 minutes
Cooking Time: 8 to 12 minutes

INGREDIENTS

1	BEATEN EGG
2	TABLESPOONS MILK
1	OZ/30 G FINE DRY BREAD CRUMBS
1	OZ/30 G FINELY CHOPPED SPRING ONION
2	TABLESPOONS CHOPPED FRESH PARSLEY
1	TEASPOON ANCHOVY PASTE
1	TEASPOON FINELY SHREDDED LEMON PEEL
1/4	TEASPOON SALT
1/4	TEASPOON PEPPER
1	LB/500 G MINCED CHICKEN
2	TABLESPOONS MARGARINE OR BUTTER

Complete the German theme by serving these patties with toasted dark bread and cooked red potatoes and onions dressed in a vinaigrette made with coarse-grain mustard.

*T*hese soft patties will be easier to shape if you wet your hands; the patties will firm up as they cook. Most supermarket meat departments or butchers will mince the chicken for you, or you may find it already prepared.

■ In a mixing bowl stir together egg, milk, bread crumbs, spring onion, parsley, anchovy paste, lemon peel, salt, and pepper. Add chicken and mix well. (Mixture will be soft.) Shape chicken mixture into four ¾-in/2 cm-thick patties.

■ In a large frying pan melt the margarine or butter. Add chicken patties and cook over medium heat for 8 to 12 minutes, or till no pink remains, turning once. Or, to grill, preheat grill and place patties on the unheated rack of a grill pan. Grill 3 to 4 in/7.5 to 10 cm from the heat for 10 to 12 minutes, turning once.

Makes 4 servings

Per serving: 224 calories, 19 g protein, 6 g carbohydrate, 13 g total fat (3 g saturated), 110 mg cholesterol, 548 mg sodium, 210 mg potassium

Stir-frying

Steps in Stir-frying Chicken

SMALL BOWLS AND
CUTTING BOARD

WOK

WOODEN SPOON

WOK SPATULA

CHEF'S KNIFE

MEASURING
SPOON

BASIC TOOLS FOR STIR-FRYING

Stir-frying uses some specialised
equipment, including a spatula-stirrer
and the flare-sided pan known as a
wok, but you can make do with a large
frying pan and a wooden spoon.

L IKE SAUTÉING, stir-frying is a quick-cooking method
using an open pan and a small amount of fat. There
are some differences, however. Sautéing, a classic French
technique, involves large pieces of meat, such as boneless
chicken breasts, cooked in a straight-sided sauté pan or a
frying pan. Stir-frying, an Asian method, requires all the
ingredients to be in small, uniform pieces; these are tossed
until done in a hot wok, a pan with deep, flared sides.

If you have ever seen a stir-fry chef in action, you know
how fast this technique can be. There isn't time to stop
between steps to slice a mushroom or mix a marinade.
Preparing ahead makes it all go smoothly, from adding
the oil to blending the sauce. Before you begin cooking,
measure, mix, cut up, and slice all the ingredients and
arrange them in bowls near the stove so they are within
easy reach.

Woks and other special equipment for stir-frying are
available from well-stocked kitchenware shops, or at
Asian markets.

similarly sized
pieces will
cook evenly
and quickly

STEP 1 **CUTTING CHICKEN CUBES OR STRIPS**
According to what the recipe calls for, cut boneless
chicken breasts or thighs into square pieces or thin
strips of approximately the same size.

cut all vegetables for
stir-frying into small,
uniform pieces

if using a large frying pan, add
the oil and tilt the pan to make
sure the oil coats the bottom
and slightly up the sides

stir-fry vegetables that need lengthy
cooking first, then add ones that
don't need as much time

STEP 2 CUTTING PEPPERS INTO STRIPS

With a medium knife, cut the pepper in half
and remove the stem, ribs, and seeds. Cut each
half into uniform lengthwise strips, then cut the
strips in half crosswise to make them bite-sized.

STEP 3 ADDING OIL TO THE WOK

Starting at the top of the pan, swirl 1 tablespoon
of oil around the sides of the wok. This allows
the oil to flow down the pan sides to coat them
completely and evenly.

STEP 4 STIR-FRYING

With a spatula or long-handled wooden spoon,
use a folding motion to gently lift and turn the
pieces of food so that each is exposed to the hot,
oil-coated cooking surface.

Stir-fried chicken and vegetables
cooked in a small amount of fat
make a light and healthy meal.
The recipe for this Pepper
Stir-fry is on page 82.

if the sauce contains
cornflour, stir it
again before adding
it to the wok

STEP 5 STIRRING IN SAUCE

When the chicken pieces are no longer pink,
push them from the centre of the wok. Pour in
the sauce and cook, stirring, until the liquid
thickens and bubbles. Return vegetables to pan.

73

Chicken Cantonese

Preparation Time: 20 minutes
Marinating Time: 30 minutes
Cooking Time: 12 to 14 minutes

INGREDIENTS

2	TABLESPOONS SOY SAUCE
1	TABLESPOON RICE WINE *OR* CHICKEN STOCK
2	TEASPOONS CORNFLOUR
12	OZ/375 G BONELESS, SKINLESS CHICKEN BREAST HALVES, CUT INTO THIN BITE-SIZED STRIPS
8	FL OZ/250 ML CHICKEN STOCK
1	TABLESPOON CORNFLOUR
6	OZ/185 G DRIED CHINESE EGG NOODLES *OR* REGULAR FINE EGG NOODLES
1	TEASPOON SESAME OIL
1	TABLESPOON COOKING OIL
2	CLOVES GARLIC, MINCED
2	TEASPOONS GRATED GINGER ROOT
2	OZ/60 G THINLY BIAS-SLICED CARROT
2	OZ/60 G THINLY BIAS-SLICED CELERY
5	OZ/155 G SLICED RED *AND/OR* GREEN PEPPER (CAPSICUM)
2-1/2	OZ/75 G CHOPPED ONION
3	OZ/90 G SLICED FRESH MUSHROOMS
2	OZ/60 G COARSELY CHOPPED ALMONDS

*T*his chicken dish is full of traditional Cantonese ingredients such as rice wine, sesame oil, and ginger. It is just as tasty served over rice instead of the egg noodles.

■ In a medium mixing bowl stir together soy sauce, rice wine or stock, and 2 teaspoons cornflour. Stir in chicken and let stand at room temperature for 30 minutes. Do not drain.

■ Meanwhile, in a small bowl stir together chicken stock and 1 tablespoon cornflour. Set aside. Cook egg noodles according to package directions; drain and return noodles to pan. Stir in sesame oil. Keep warm.

■ Pour cooking oil into a wok or large frying pan. (Add more oil as necessary during cooking.) Preheat over medium-high heat. Stir-fry garlic and ginger root in hot oil for 15 seconds. Add carrot; stir-fry for 1 minute. Add celery and stir-fry for 1 minute. Add pepper and onion; stir-fry for 1 minute. Add mushrooms; stir-fry for 1 minute more, or till vegetables are crisp-tender. Remove all vegetables from wok.

■ Add almonds to hot wok; stir-fry for 2 to 3 minutes, or till toasted. Remove from wok. Add undrained chicken to hot wok; stir-fry for 3 to 4 minutes, or till tender and no pink remains. Push chicken from centre of wok. Stir chicken stock–cornflour mixture; add to centre of wok. Cook and stir till thickened and bubbly. Return vegetables and almonds to wok. Stir all ingredients together to coat with sauce. Cook and stir about 1 minute more, or till heated through. Serve over noodles.

Makes 4 servings

Per serving: 427 calories, 27 g protein, 42 g carbohydrate, 17 g total fat (3 g saturated), 82 mg cholesterol, 735 mg sodium, 552 mg potassium

STEPS AT A GLANCE	Page
SKINNING & BONING CHICKEN	10
PREPARING STIR-FRY INGREDIENTS	74
STIR-FRYING CHICKEN	72

74

STEPS IN PREPARING STIR-FRY INGREDIENTS

STEP 1 BIAS-SLICING CARROTS
Hold a chef's knife at a 45-degree angle to the peeled carrot and make the first cut. Make evenly spaced cuts at the same angle the entire length.

STEP 2 GRATING GINGER
Cut a slice off one edge of an unpeeled piece of ginger root to remove the woody end. Hold the ginger root at a 45-degree angle to a ginger grater or fine grater and rub across the grating surface.

Serve this main course in the authentic
Chinese style over noodles on
a platter, with big chopsticks
(or tongs) for serving.

Stir-fried nuggets of chicken are combined with broccoli florets in this homemade version of a Chinese restaurant favourite.

76

Crystal Chicken with Broccoli

Preparation Time: 40 minutes
Cooking Time: 10 to 12 minutes

INGREDIENTS

4	OZ/125 G PLAIN FLOUR
1/4	TEASPOON BAKING POWDER
6	FL OZ/180 ML WATER
2	TABLESPOONS SOY SAUCE
2	CLOVES GARLIC, FLATTENED
3	FL OZ/90 ML HONEY
2	TABLESPOONS SOY SAUCE
2	TABLESPOONS CIDER VINEGAR
2	TABLESPOONS MOLASSES OR GOLDEN SYRUP
2	TABLESPOONS WATER
2	TABLESPOONS DRY SHERRY
2	CLOVES GARLIC, MINCED
2	TEASPOONS CORNFLOUR
12	OZ/375 G BONELESS, SKINLESS CHICKEN BREAST HALVES
	COOKING OIL FOR DEEP-FAT FRYING
1	TABLESPOON COOKING OIL
6	OZ/185 G BROCCOLI FLORETS

*T*o vary the colours and flavours of this dish, use 6 oz/ 185 g mixed vegetables in place of the broccoli. Red peppers (capsicums), carrots, and asparagus are good choices.

■ In a medium mixing bowl stir together flour, baking powder, 6 fl oz/180 ml water, 2 tablespoons soy sauce, and flattened garlic; let stand for 15 minutes. Discard garlic.

■ Meanwhile, in a small mixing bowl combine honey, 2 tablespoons soy sauce, vinegar, molasses or golden syrup, 2 tablespoons water, dry sherry, minced garlic, and cornflour; set aside. Rinse chicken; pat dry. Cut chicken into 1½ x ½-in/ 4-cmx12-mm strips. Add to flour batter.

■ In a wok or 2-qt/2-l saucepan heat 2 in/5 cm of oil to 365°F/ 185°C. Remove chicken from flour batter, allowing excess to drain off. Fry chicken strips, a few pieces at a time, in hot oil for 30 to 60 seconds, or till golden. Drain on paper towels.

■ Pour 1 tablespoon cooking oil into a large frying pan. (Add more oil if necessary during cooking.) Preheat over medium-high heat. Add the broccoli and stir-fry for 4 to 5 minutes, or till crisp-tender. Arrange broccoli around the edge of a serving platter; keep warm.

■ Stir honey-soy mixture; add to the frying pan. Cook and stir till thickened and bubbly. Cook and stir for 1 minute more. Return cooked chicken to frying pan; heat through. Pour chicken and sauce into centre of broccoli-lined serving platter.

Makes 4 servings

Per serving: 527 calories, 25 g protein, 69 g carbohydrate, 17 g total fat (3 g saturated), 45 mg cholesterol, 765 mg sodium, 659 mg potassium

STEPS AT A GLANCE	Page
SKINNING & BONING CHICKEN	10
TRIMMING BROCCOLI & DEEP-FRYING CHICKEN	77
STIR-FRYING CHICKEN	72

STEPS IN TRIMMING BROCCOLI AND DEEP-FRYING CHICKEN

STEP 1 **BROCCOLI FLORETS**

Cut away the florets from the stalk with a paring knife. Halve large pieces so all the florets are similar in size.

STEP 2 **DEEP-FRYING CHICKEN**

Pour oil into a wok or saucepan; heat to 365°F/185°C (test with a deep-fat thermometer). Drain chicken of excess batter and fry, a few pieces at a time, until golden. Lift out with a slotted spoon; drain on paper towels.

Thai-Style Chicken & Spinach

Look for coriander and fish sauce, the distinctive flavours in this dish, in a well-stocked supermarket or Asian grocer.

Preparation Time: 20 minutes
Cooking Time: 8 to 10 minutes

INGREDIENTS

2	FL OZ/60 ML CHICKEN STOCK
1	TABLESPOON FISH SAUCE *OR* 2 TEASPOONS SOY SAUCE
1	TABLESPOON CORNFLOUR
2	TABLESPOONS CHOPPED FRESH CORIANDER (CHINESE PARSLEY)
12	OZ/375 G BONELESS, SKINLESS CHICKEN THIGHS, CUT INTO 1-IN/2.5-CM PIECES
1	TABLESPOON HOT CHILI OIL *OR* SESAME OIL WITH A DASH OF DRIED CHILI POWDER
1-1/4	LB/625 G SPINACH LEAVES, WASHED AND TRIMMED
3	CLOVES GARLIC, MINCED
2	OZ/60 G CHOPPED PEANUTS

78

*T*wo special ingredients give this dish its unique flavour. Thai fish sauce, or nam pla, is a fermented liquid with a rich flavour. If you prefer a milder dish, substitute peanut oil for the hot chili oil.

■ In a small bowl combine chicken stock, fish sauce or soy sauce, and cornflour; set aside.

■ In a large mixing bowl toss coriander with chicken. Pour hot chili oil into a wok or large frying pan. Preheat over medium-high heat. Stir-fry chicken for 2 to 3 minutes, or till no pink remains. Remove the chicken from the wok.

■ Add spinach and garlic to wok; toss to mix. Return chicken to the wok. Reduce heat to medium-low; cover and cook for 3 minutes. Push chicken and vegetables from centre of wok to the sides of the pan.

■ Stir chicken stock mixture; add to centre of the wok. Cook and stir till thickened and bubbly. Stir all ingredients together to coat with sauce; cook for 1 minute more. Spoon mixture into a serving bowl and sprinkle with chopped peanuts.

Makes 4 servings

Per serving: 352 calories, 26 g protein, 38 g carbohydrate, 11 g total fat (2 g saturated), 45 mg cholesterol, 395 mg sodium, 1,050 mg potassium

STEPS AT A GLANCE	Page
SKINNING & BONING CHICKEN	10
STIR-FRYING CHICKEN	72

Sesame Chicken with Vegetables

STEPS AT A GLANCE	Page
SKINNING & BONING CHICKEN	10
DEEP-FRYING CHICKEN	77
STIR-FRYING CHICKEN	72

Preparation Time: 20 minutes
Cooking Time: about 25 minutes

INGREDIENTS

SAUCE

4	FL OZ/125 ML CHICKEN STOCK
2	TABLESPOONS SOY SAUCE
1	TABLESPOON SESAME OIL
4	CLOVES GARLIC, MINCED
2	TO 3 TEASPOONS GRATED GINGER ROOT
2	TEASPOONS CORNFLOUR
1	TEASPOON SUGAR

CHICKEN

2	OZ/60 G PLAIN FLOUR
2	TABLESPOONS SESAME SEEDS
1/2	TEASPOON SALT
1/4	TEASPOON GROUND RED (CAYENNE) PEPPER
1	BEATEN EGG
2	FL OZ/60 ML MILK
	COOKING OIL FOR DEEP-FAT FRYING
1	LB/500 G BONELESS, SKINLESS CHICKEN THIGHS, CUT INTO 3/4-IN/2-CM PIECES

VEGETABLES

1	TABLESPOON COOKING OIL
2	ZUCCHINI (COURGETTES), CUT INTO THIN, BITE-SIZED STRIPS
1	GREEN PEPPER (CAPSICUM), CUT INTO THIN, BITE-SIZED STRIPS
6	SPRING ONIONS, BIAS-SLICED INTO 1/2-IN/12-MM PIECES

*T*o deep-fry the chicken pieces, follow the procedure shown on page 77. When mixing the fried pieces with the sauce at the end, don't cook them too long or the coating may become soggy.

■ For sauce, in a small bowl stir together chicken stock, soy sauce, sesame oil, garlic, ginger root, cornflour, and sugar. Set aside.

■ For chicken, in a large mixing bowl combine flour, sesame seeds, salt, and ground red pepper. In a small mixing bowl combine egg and milk. Add to dry ingredients and beat till smooth. In a wok or 2-qt/2-l saucepan heat 1¼ in/3 cm cooking oil to 365°F/185°C. Dip chicken, 1 piece at a time, into the coating, then add to hot oil. Fry chicken, a few pieces at a time, about 4 minutes, or till golden. Using a slotted spoon, remove chicken from oil. Drain on paper towels. Keep warm in a preheated 300°F/150°C oven.

■ For vegetables, pour cooking oil into a large frying pan. (Add more oil if necessary during cooking.) Preheat over medium-high heat. Stir-fry zucchini (courgettes), green pepper, and spring onions for 3 minutes, or till crisp-tender. Push vegetables from the centre of the pan. Stir sauce; add to the pan. Cook and stir till thickened and bubbly. Cook for 1 minute more. Return the cooked chicken to the pan. Stir all ingredients together to coat with sauce. Serve immediately.

Makes 6 servings

Per serving: 359 calories, 19 g protein, 14 g carbohydrate, 25 g total fat (4 g saturated), 76 mg cholesterol, 617 mg sodium, 359 mg potassium

79

Arrange stir-fried chicken and vegetables around a mound of hot cooked rice that has been moulded in a bowl and inverted onto the platter. Garnish with lemon, sesame seeds, and spring onion tops.

Sweet & Sour Chicken

*W*e used salted dry biscuit crumbs instead of the customary batter to coat the chicken pieces for this perennial favourite. This not only decreases the preparation time, it reduces the fat content of the finished dish as well.

■ Drain pineapple, reserving 6 fl oz/180 ml juice. In a small bowl stir together the reserved pineapple juice, the ketchup, 1 tablespoon cornflour, vinegar, water, and sugar. Set aside.

■ In a medium mixing bowl stir together egg and 1 tablespoon cornflour till smooth. Add chicken pieces and stir to coat chicken with egg mixture. Pour biscuit crumbs into a shallow dish. Roll chicken pieces in crumbs to coat evenly.

■ Pour cooking oil into a wok or large frying pan. (Add more oil if necessary during cooking.) Preheat over medium-high heat. Add half of the chicken to the wok. Stir-fry about 3 minutes, or till no pink remains. Remove chicken and keep warm in a preheated 300°F/150°C oven. Repeat with remaining chicken.

■ Add peppers and spring onions to wok; stir-fry for 2 to 3 minutes, or till crisp-tender. Remove vegetables from wok.

■ Stir pineapple juice mixture; add to the centre of the wok. Cook and stir till thickened and bubbly. Cook and stir for 2 minutes more. Return chicken, vegetables, and pineapple chunks to wok. Stir all ingredients together to coat with sauce. Cook and stir about 1 minute more, or till heated through. If desired, serve with rice.

Makes 4 servings

Per serving: 334 calories, 20 g protein, 42 g carbohydrate, 9 g total fat (2 g saturated), 100 mg cholesterol, 467 mg sodium, 459 mg potassium

STEPS AT A GLANCE	Page
SKINNING & BONING CHICKEN	10
STIR-FRYING CHICKEN	72

Preparation Time: 20 minutes
Cooking Time: 12 to 14 minutes

INGREDIENTS

1	LB/500 G TINNED PINEAPPLE CHUNKS, INCLUDING JUICE
2	FL OZ/60 ML KETCHUP (TOMATO SAUCE)
1	TABLESPOON CORNFLOUR
2	TABLESPOONS RED WINE VINEGAR
2	TABLESPOONS WATER
4	TEASPOONS SUGAR
1	BEATEN EGG
1	TABLESPOON CORNFLOUR
12	OZ/375 G BONELESS, SKINLESS CHICKEN BREAST HALVES, CUT INTO 1-IN/2.5-CM CUBES
2	OZ/60 G FINELY CRUSHED SALTINE BISCUITS OR LIGHTLY SALTED DRY BISCUITS
1	TABLESPOON COOKING OIL
1	GREEN PEPPER (CAPSICUM), CUT INTO 1/2-IN/12-MM PIECES
1	RED PEPPER (CAPSICUM), CUT INTO 1/2-IN/12-MM PIECES
4	SPRING ONIONS, BIAS-SLICED INTO 1-1/2-IN/4-CM PIECES
	HOT COOKED RICE (OPTIONAL)

An Oriental platter accentuates the hues and flavours of this classic Chinese recipe.

80

Stir-fried Chicken Thighs with Fresh Asparagus

Preparation Time: 20 minutes
Marinating Time: 20 to 30 minutes
Cooking Time: 12 to 14 minutes

A bowl of rice with a colourful blend of chicken and vegetables, and chop-sticks for utensils add up to an authentic Asian feast.

INGREDIENTS

1	LIGHTLY BEATEN EGG WHITE
1	TABLESPOON CORNFLOUR
1	TABLESPOON DRY WHITE WINE
1	CLOVE GARLIC, MINCED
1/4	TEASPOON SALT
1/4	TEASPOON WHITE PEPPER
1	LB/500 G BONELESS, SKINLESS CHICKEN THIGHS, CUT INTO THIN BITE-SIZED STRIPS
2	TABLESPOONS CHILI SAUCE
2	TABLESPOONS SOY SAUCE
1	TABLESPOON WINE VINEGAR
1	TO 1-1/2 TEASPOONS CHILI OIL OR SESAME OIL WITH A DASH OF DRIED CHILI POWDER
1	TABLESPOON COOKING OIL
1	LB/500 G ASPARAGUS SPEARS, BIAS-SLICED INTO 2-IN/5-CM PIECES
1	RED PEPPER (CAPSICUM), CUT INTO BITE-SIZED STRIPS
4	SPRING ONIONS, BIAS-SLICED INTO 1-IN/2.5-CM PIECES

81

*W*hile the chicken is marinating, prepare the sauce and vegetables. After cleaning the asparagus, hold each spear in one hand and bend it gently until the end snaps off; discard ends.

■ In a medium mixing bowl stir together the egg white, cornflour, wine, garlic, salt, and white pepper. Stir in the chicken strips. Cover and let stand at room temperature for 20 to 30 minutes. Do not drain. Meanwhile, in a small bowl stir together chili sauce, soy sauce, wine vinegar, and chili oil. Set aside.

■ Pour cooking oil into a wok or large frying pan. (Add more oil if necessary during cooking.) Preheat over medium-high heat. Stir-fry half the asparagus, pepper, and spring onions for 3 to 4 minutes, or till crisp-tender. Remove from wok. Repeat with the remaining vegetables.

■ Add undrained chicken strips to hot wok. Stir-fry for 3 to 4 minutes, or till no pink remains. Return cooked vegetables to wok. Stir chili sauce mixture; stir into chicken and vegetables. Cover wok and cook about 1 minute more, or till heated through.

Makes 4 servings

Per serving: 216 calories, 20 g protein, 10 g carbohydrate, 11 g total fat (2 g saturated), 54 mg cholesterol, 765 mg sodium, 497 mg potassium

STEPS AT A GLANCE	Page
SKINNING & BONING CHICKEN	10
STIR-FRYING CHICKEN	72

Pepper Stir-fry

Preparation Time: 20 minutes
Cooking Time: 8 to 10 minutes

INGREDIENTS

8	FL OZ/250 ML CHICKEN STOCK
2	TABLESPOONS PLAIN FLOUR
2	TABLESPOONS TOMATO PASTE
1/2	TEASPOON PAPRIKA
1/4	TEASPOON SALT
1/4	TEASPOON PEPPER
1	TABLESPOON COOKING OIL
1	LARGE ONION, CUT INTO THIN WEDGES
3	OZ/90 G SLICED FRESH MUSHROOMS
1	MEDIUM GREEN PEPPER (CAPSICUM), CUT INTO THIN, BITE-SIZED STRIPS
1	MEDIUM RED PEPPER (CAPSICUM), CUT INTO THIN, BITE-SIZED STRIPS
12	OZ/375 G BONELESS, SKINLESS CHICKEN THIGHS, CUT INTO BITE-SIZED STRIPS
1	TABLESPOON DRAINED CAPERS OR 2 TABLESPOONS CHOPPED DILL PICKLE (OPTIONAL)
	HOT COOKED PASTA OR RICE

Corkscrew pasta, or rotelle, makes the perfect base for a stir-fry with European flavours.

STEPS AT A GLANCE	Page
SKINNING & BONING CHICKEN	10
STIR-FRYING CHICKEN	72

*H*ere's a stir-fry recipe with Mediterranean influences. The capers give this quickly-prepared dish an unexpected tang.

■ In a small bowl stir together the chicken stock, flour, tomato paste, paprika, salt, and pepper. Set aside.

■ Pour cooking oil into a wok or large frying pan. (Add more oil if necessary during cooking.) Preheat over medium-high heat. Stir-fry onion for 1½ minutes. Add mushrooms; stir-fry for 1 to 2 minutes, or till tender. Remove onion and mushrooms from wok.

■ Add green and red peppers; stir-fry for about 1½ minutes, or till peppers are crisp-tender. Remove from wok. Add chicken strips; stir-fry for 2 to 3 minutes, or till no pink remains. Push chicken from centre of wok. Stir chicken stock mixture; add sauce to the centre of the wok. Cook and stir till thickened and bubbly.

■ Return vegetables to wok. If desired, add capers or dill pickle. Stir all ingredients together to coat with sauce. Cook and stir about 1 minute more, or till heated through. Serve over pasta or rice.

Makes 4 servings

Per serving: 299 calories, 19 g protein, 36 g carbohydrate, 9 g total fat (2 g saturated), 41 mg cholesterol, 378 mg sodium, 509 mg potassium

Ginger Chicken with Peas & Shiitakes

Although you'll pay more for shiitake mushrooms, their flavour is woodier and richer than white mushrooms and well worth the extra expense. Many supermarkets and greengrocers carry a wide selection of fresh mushrooms.

■ In a medium saucepan cook snow peas and green peas in boiling water for 1 minute, or till pea pods are crisp-tender. Drain and set aside.

■ In a bowl stir together light cream, cornflour, salt, and pepper. Set aside.

■ Pour oil into a wok or large frying pan. (Add more oil if necessary during cooking.) Preheat over medium-high heat. Stir-fry ginger root in hot oil for 30 seconds. Add mushrooms; stir-fry for about 2 minutes, or till tender. Remove vegetables from wok.

■ Add chicken strips to hot wok. Stir-fry for 3 to 4 minutes, or till no pink remains. Push chicken from centre of wok. Stir cream mixture; add to the centre of wok. Cook and stir till thickened and bubbly. Return cooked vegetables and parsley to wok. Stir all ingredients together to coat with sauce. Cook and stir for 1 minute more, or till heated through. Sprinkle with parsley.

Makes 4 servings

Per serving: 263 calories, 22 g protein, 21 g carbohydrate, 11 g total fat (4 g saturated), 59 mg cholesterol, 352 mg sodium, 486 mg potassium

Preparation Time: 20 minutes
Cooking Time: 10 to 12 minutes

STEPS AT A GLANCE	Page
SKINNING & BONING CHICKEN	10
STIR-FRYING CHICKEN	72

INGREDIENTS

5	OZ/155 G FRESH SNOW PEAS (MANGETOUTS), TIPS AND STRINGS REMOVED
5	OZ/155 G FROZEN PEAS
6	FL OZ/180 ML LIGHT (SINGLE) CREAM
2	TEASPOONS CORNFLOUR
1/2	TEASPOON SALT
1/8	TEASPOON PEPPER
1	TABLESPOON COOKING OIL
2	TEASPOONS GRATED FRESH GINGER ROOT
8	OZ/250 G FRESH SHIITAKE MUSHROOMS *OR* OTHER MUSHROOMS, STEMS REMOVED AND SLICED
12	OZ/375 G BONELESS, SKINLESS CHICKEN BREAST HALVES, CUT INTO THIN BITE-SIZED STRIPS
1/2	OZ/15 G CHOPPED FRESH PARSLEY

83

Not all stir-fry dishes are created equal: this one contains shiitake mushrooms, peas, and a cream sauce. Serve on steamed barley or rice.

Chicken with Artichokes

STEPS AT A GLANCE Page

SKINNING & BONING
CHICKEN 10

STIR-FRYING CHICKEN 72

Add a bit more of the crushed hot pepper (chili) flakes to this dish if you like your food a little spicier. You can substitute blanched small fresh artichokes that have been trimmed of outer leaves, thorny tops, and fuzzy chokes for the frozen or tinned artichokes.

■ In a small bowl, stir together chicken broth, Worcestershire sauce, oregano, thyme, cornflour, and crushed red pepper. Set aside.

■ In a wok or large frying pan cook the bacon till crisp; drain on paper towels. Drain fat. Wipe wok or pan clean with paper towels. Pour cooking oil into wok. Preheat over medium-high heat. Stir-fry garlic in hot oil for 15 seconds. Add pepper and onion; stir-fry for 2 minutes, or till crisp-tender. Remove from wok.

■ Add chicken to hot wok. Stir-fry for 2 to 3 minutes, or till no pink remains. Push chicken from centre of wok. Stir chicken stock mixture; add to the centre of wok. Cook and stir till thickened and bubbly. Return cooked vegetables to wok. Add thawed artichokes. Stir all ingredients together to coat with sauce. Cook and stir for about 2 minutes more, or till heated through. Sprinkle with bacon pieces.

Makes 4 servings

Fresh herbal flavours and chunky vegetables give this stir-fry recipe a decidedly Western character. Try it with *penne* pasta or macaroni.

Per serving: 212 calories, 21 g protein, 14 g carbohydrate, 9 g total fat (2 g saturated), 49 mg cholesterol, 314 mg sodium, 510 mg potassium

84

Preparation Time: 20 minutes
Cooking Time: 10 to 12 minutes

INGREDIENTS

4	OZ/125 ML CHICKEN STOCK
1	TABLESPOON WORCESTERSHIRE SAUCE
1	TABLESPOON CHOPPED FRESH OREGANO *OR* 1 TEASPOON DRIED OREGANO, CRUSHED
2	TEASPOONS CHOPPED FRESH THYME *OR* 1/2 TEASPOON DRIED THYME, CRUSHED
2	TEASPOONS CORNFLOUR
1/8	TEASPOON CRUSHED HOT PEPPER (CHILI) FLAKES
3	SLICES BACON, CUT INTO 1/2-IN/12-MM PIECES
1	TABLESPOON COOKING OIL
2	CLOVES GARLIC, MINCED
1	RED PEPPER (CAPSICUM), CUT INTO 3/4-IN/2-CM PIECES
1	MEDIUM ONION, THINLY SLICED AND SEPARATED INTO RINGS
12	OZ/375 G BONELESS, SKINLESS CHICKEN BREAST HALVES *OR* THIGHS, CUT INTO BITE-SIZED PIECES
9	OZ/280 G TINNED *OR* THAWED FROZEN ARTICHOKE HEARTS

Braising

Steps in Braising Chicken

LARGE FRYING PAN
AND LID

MEASURING CUP

TONGS

BASIC TOOLS FOR BRAISING

Braised or stewed chicken will stay moist and juicy if simmered in a heavy frying pan with a snug-fitting lid. Use tongs to move chicken pieces and a measuring cup for adding liquid to the pan.

BRAISING COMBINES two cooking techniques. First the meat is sautéed in a little fat to develop its colour and flavour, then it is slowly cooked in a small amount of liquid — just enough to keep it succulent and later to serve as the base for a sauce — in a covered pan, either on top of the stove or in the oven.

Stewing is almost the same as braising, except that the meat may not always be browned first and much more cooking liquid is used. Meat for stews is usually cut into smaller pieces than meat for braising.

Although the cooking time is long compared to rapid methods like stir-fries or sautés, braising and stewing make few demands on the cook other than to check the heat occasionally to regulate the temperature or to see if the cooking liquid needs replenishing. In fact, both braised dishes and stews are ideal fare for entertaining because they keep well and actually improve in flavour by sitting. Any fat can then be skimmed from the surface. To serve, simply reheat.

Another attraction is that braised dishes may be almost complete meals. Most have vegetables cooked with the meat. All that is needed are accompaniments like noodles, rice, or potatoes to soak up the sauce. A braised dish also can be an excellent choice for low-fat diets, as the chicken can be skinned without the risk of it drying out in cooking. To skin chicken prior to braising, see pages 10 and 11.

When browning chicken (the first step in braising), don't crowd the pieces or they won't develop good colour; see pages 52 and 53 for more information on proper sautéing technique. Use a heavy pan with a lid. You can brown the chicken in one pan and then simmer it in another, but you will lose all the delicious bits that stick to the bottom of the pan and add so much flavour to any sauce. For braised dishes that finish cooking in the oven, be sure that the cooking pot is safe for both stovetop and oven use. A flameproof casserole dish or other heavy pan with a tight-fitting lid holds in the juices best.

the bits left over from browning the chicken add richness to the cooking liquid

a braised dish uses more liquid than a sauté, and a stew uses more liquid still

STEP 1 BROWNING CHICKEN

Add oil to the pan and brown the chicken breast halves or other chicken pieces over medium heat. Using tongs, turn the pieces and brown them on the other side. Remove from the pan.

STEP 2 ADDING LIQUID TO THE PAN

After any other ingredients have been briefly sautéed, return the chicken to the pan and pour in the cooking liquid so that it is evenly distributed around the food.

at a simmer, bubbles will form slowly and break just below the surface

STEP 3 SIMMERING THE INGREDIENTS

Bring the liquid to a boil, then reduce heat. Cover and simmer until the chicken is tender and cooked through. Sometimes the final simmering is done in the oven. If so, use a pan with heatproof handles and lid. Or, wrap the lid and handles with heavy-duty foil.

Succulent, tasty Braised Chicken with Apple-Cream Sauce (see page 99) epitomises the delicious art of braising.

In France, this rich, pungent dish is
usually served with parsleyed potatoes
to soak up some of its delicious gravy.

Hearty Coq au Vin

STEPS AT A GLANCE	Page
MAKING CROUTONS	89
BRAISING CHICKEN	86

Preparation Time: 25 minutes
Baking Time: 1 hour

INGREDIENTS

CROUTONS

4	SLICES FRENCH BREAD
4	TEASPOONS OLIVE OIL
1	CLOVE GARLIC, HALVED

COQ AU VIN

2	TO 2-1/2 LB/1 TO 1.25 KG MEATY CHICKEN PIECES (BREASTS, THIGHS, AND DRUMSTICKS)
1	TABLESPOON MARGARINE OR BUTTER
1	TABLESPOON COOKING OIL
	SALT
	PEPPER
4-1/2	OZ/140 G FRESH MUSHROOMS, CUT INTO QUARTERS
12	PEARL OR PICKLING ONIONS, PEELED
2	SLICES BACON, CUT UP
2	CLOVES GARLIC, MINCED
2	TABLESPOONS PLAIN FLOUR
8	FL OZ/250 ML CHICKEN STOCK
8	FL OZ/250 ML DRY RED WINE
2	TABLESPOONS TOMATO PASTE
1	TOMATO, PEELED, SEEDED, AND CHOPPED
1	TABLESPOON CHOPPED FRESH PARSLEY
1	TABLESPOON CHOPPED FRESH TARRAGON OR 1 TEASPOON DRIED TARRAGON, CRUSHED
1	BAY LEAF
2	TABLESPOONS CHOPPED FRESH PARSLEY

*T*his traditional French recipe may be made with white wine, but a deep red-wine flavour has become its hallmark. It is an ideal way to use the last glass in an unfinished bottle.

■ For croutons, lightly brush both sides of French bread slices with olive oil. Rub with cut side of garlic clove. Cut bread slices into ¾- to 1-in/2- to 2.5-cm pieces. Place the bread cubes in a shallow baking pan. Bake in a preheated 300°F/150°C oven for about 15 minutes or till crisp, stirring once. Set 1½ oz/ 45 g of the croutons aside till serving time. Cover and store remaining croutons for another use.

■ For coq au vin, skin chicken, if desired. Rinse chicken; pat dry. In a heavy cooking pot or flameproof casserole dish brown chicken pieces on all sides in hot margarine or butter and oil. Remove chicken from pot; sprinkle with salt and pepper.

■ In the same pot cook mushrooms, onions, bacon, and garlic till tender. Drain off fat, reserving 2 tablespoons in pot. Stir flour into reserved fat and cook for 1 minute. Add chicken stock, wine, tomato paste, chopped tomato, 1 tablespoon parsley, tarragon, and bay leaf. Return chicken pieces to pot; bring to boiling. Cover and bake in a preheated 350°F/180°C oven for 45 minutes. Remove bay leaf. If necessary, skim off excess fat. Top each serving with some of the croutons and 2 tablespoons chopped parsley.

Makes 4 servings

Per serving: 491 calories, 39 g protein, 17 g carbohydrate, 25 g total fat (6 g saturated), 107 mg cholesterol, 615 mg sodium, 715 mg potassium

STEPS IN MAKING CROUTONS

STEP 1 **RUBBING BREAD WITH GARLIC**

Slice French bread 1 in/2.5 cm thick. Brush the slices with olive oil. Halve a clove of garlic and rub it across both sides of the bread slices.

STEP 2 **CUTTING CROUTONS**

Cut the coated bread slices in ¾- to 1-in/2- to 2.5-cm strips with a serrated knife; don't separate the strips. Then hold the knife crosswise to the strips and slice again, creating ¾- to 1-in/2- to 2.5-cm cubes.

Alsatian-Style Chicken & Dumplings

INGREDIENTS

CHICKEN

2	TO 2-1/2 LB/1 TO 1.25 KG MEATY CHICKEN PIECES (BREASTS, THIGHS, AND DRUMSTICKS)
1	TABLESPOON COOKING OIL
2	OZ/60 G CHOPPED ONION
18	OZ/510 G FIRMLY PACKED SHREDDED CABBAGE
15	OZ/425 G TINNED DICED TOMATOES
4	OZ/125 G CHOPPED GREEN PEPPER (CAPSICUM)
1	TO 2 TABLESPOONS BROWN SUGAR
1	TEASPOON CARAWAY SEED
1/4	TEASPOON SALT
1/8	TEASPOON PEPPER
8	FL OZ/250 ML DRY WHITE WINE, OR APPLE JUICE OR APPLE CIDER
8	FL OZ/250 ML CHICKEN STOCK

DUMPLINGS

1-1/2	OZ/45 G PLAIN FLOUR
2	OZ/60 G POLENTA OR CORNMEAL
1	TEASPOON BAKING POWDER
1/4	TEASPOON SALT
3	FL OZ/90 ML MILK
2	TABLESPOONS COOKING OIL
2	PIECES BACON, CRISP-COOKED AND CRUMBLED
1	TABLESPOON CHOPPED FRESH PARSLEY

I *f you substitute apple juice or cider for the wine, use 1 tablespoon of brown sugar rather than 2, since the cider is already sweetened.*

■ For chicken, skin chicken pieces, if desired. Rinse chicken; pat dry. In a 4½-qt/4.5-l heavy cooking pot or flameproof casserole dish brown chicken in hot oil on all sides over medium heat. Remove from pot. Add onion to pot and cook for 2 to 3 minutes, or till crisp-tender. Add cabbage, tomatoes (undrained), green pepper, brown sugar, caraway seed, ¼ teaspoon salt, and pepper. Stir in wine, apple juice, or apple cider. Bring mixture to boiling; return chicken pieces to pot. Reduce heat; cover and simmer for 30 minutes. Stir in chicken stock; return mixture to boiling.

■ Meanwhile, for dumplings, in a medium mixing bowl stir together the flour, polenta or cornmeal, baking powder, and salt. In another bowl combine milk and 2 tablespoons cooking oil; add to dry ingredients and stir with a fork till combined. Stir in bacon and parsley. Drop flour mixture from a tablespoon to make 6 mounds atop the hot, bubbling stew. Cover and simmer for 10 to 12 minutes, or till a toothpick inserted in the centre of a dumpling comes out clean. Do not lift cover during cooking. If desired, garnish with additional chopped parsley.

Makes 6 servings

Per serving: 394 calories, 28 g protein, 25 g carbohydrate, 18 g total fat (4 g saturated), 72 mg cholesterol, 550 mg sodium, 704 mg potassium

Preparation Time: 30 minutes
Cooking Time: 40 to 42 minutes

STEPS AT A GLANCE	Page
SKINNING CHICKEN	10–11
BRAISING CHICKEN	86
MAKING DUMPLINGS	90

90

STEPS IN MAKING DUMPLINGS

STEP 1 **MIXING DUMPLINGS**

Add milk mixture to flour mixture and stir with a fork until the dry ingredients are barely moistened; don't overmix or the dumplings will be tough.

STEP 2 **DROPPING DUMPLINGS**

Scoop up 1 tablespoon of dumpling batter and drop in a mound onto the hot, bubbling liquid. Use a second spoon or rubber spatula to ease the batter off the tablespoon.

STEP 3 **TESTING FOR DONENESS**

To test the dumplings for doneness, insert a toothpick into the thickest part of one; if it comes out clean, the dumplings are ready.

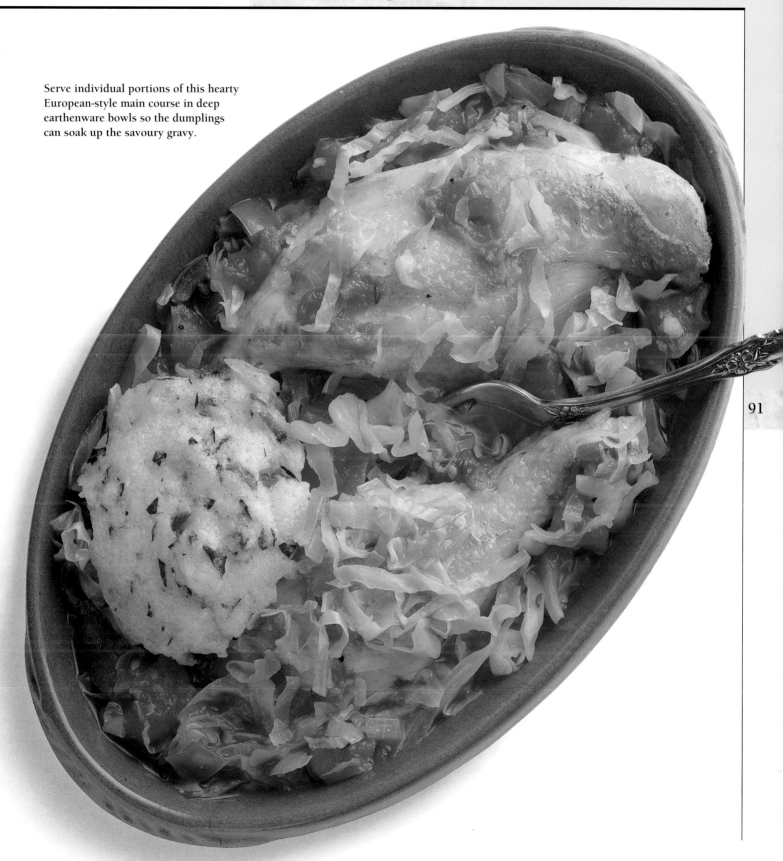

Serve individual portions of this hearty European-style main course in deep earthenware bowls so the dumplings can soak up the savoury gravy.

Chicken with Spicy Yogurt Sauce

STEPS AT A GLANCE	Page
SKINNING DRUMSTICKS OR LEGS	11
SCORING & MARINATING CHICKEN	92
BRAISING CHICKEN	86

*P*aprika, though often used just for a touch of colour, can be quite tasty. Using fine-quality paprika, such as the imported Hungarian type, can make all the difference in a dish like this.

■ Rinse chicken; pat dry. Lightly score the flesh of the chicken. Place chicken in a large plastic bag set into a shallow dish. In a small mixing bowl stir together yogurt, coriander or parsley, curry powder, garlic, ginger, paprika, lime or lemon juice, and salt. Pour yogurt mixture over chicken. Seal bag; turn bag to coat chicken with marinade. Marinate in the refrigerator for 2 to 24 hours, turning bag occasionally.

■ In a large frying pan melt the margarine or butter over medium heat. Add the chicken legs and the yogurt mixture. Bring to boiling; reduce heat. Cover and simmer for 45 to 50 minutes, or till chicken is tender and no pink remains. Transfer chicken to a serving platter. Boil yogurt mixture gently for about 5 minutes, or till slightly thickened. If desired, garnish with coriander or parsley.

Makes 4 servings

Per serving: 275 calories, 29 g protein, 6 g carbohydrate, 15 g total fat (4 g saturated), 91 mg cholesterol, 480 mg sodium, 409 mg potassium

Preparation Time: 15 minutes
Marinating Time: 2 to 24 hours
Cooking Time: 50 to 55 minutes

INGREDIENTS

4	WHOLE CHICKEN LEGS (DRUMSTICK PLUS THIGH), SKIN REMOVED
8	OZ/250 G PLAIN LOW-FAT YOGURT
2	TABLESPOONS CHOPPED FRESH CORIANDER (CHINESE PARSLEY) OR PARSLEY
1	TABLESPOON CURRY POWDER
2	CLOVES GARLIC, MINCED
1	TEASPOON GROUND GINGER
1	TEASPOON PAPRIKA
2	TO 3 TEASPOONS LIME JUICE OR LEMON JUICE
1/2	TEASPOON SALT
2	TABLESPOONS MARGARINE OR BUTTER
	FRESH CORIANDER (CHINESE PARSLEY) OR PARSLEY (OPTIONAL)

92

STEPS IN SCORING & MARINATING CHICKEN

STEP 1 SCORING CHICKEN

First remove skin from the chicken legs. Then make shallow parallel marks in the meatiest section of each leg with a chef's knife. These cuts allow the marinade to penetrate the meat.

STEP 2 MARINATING CHICKEN

Combine the marinade ingredients in a small bowl, then transfer to a heavy-duty plastic bag large enough to hold all the chicken pieces. Add the chicken, seal the bag, and turn several times to coat. Lay the bag on its side in a shallow baking dish or bowl. This method works with any marinade and any cooking method.

STEP 3 TURNING THE BAG

As the chicken marinates, turn the bag several times so that the pieces are immersed in the marinade. This way the juices penetrate all the pieces evenly.

To serve, cover each chicken leg
generously with sauce. Accompany
with pita bread (Middle Eastern flat
bread) and sautéed vegetables.

Chicken Mole

*T*he word mole *comes from an American Indian word meaning "concoction" and applies to a variety of blended Mexican sauces that are particularly tasty with chicken and turkey. One of the most famous variations includes a small amount of dark chocolate.*

■ Rinse chicken; pat dry. Heat 1 tablespoon of the cooking oil in a 12-in/30-cm heavy frying pan. Add onion and garlic and cook for 3 to 5 minutes, or till onion is tender but not brown. Remove from frying pan and cool slightly.

■ In a blender container or food processor bowl combine onion mixture, tomatillos, tomato purée, almonds, tortilla chips, water, chilies, coriander, sesame seeds, cinnamon, salt, and cloves. Blend or process till smooth.

■ Heat remaining oil in frying pan. Add chicken and cook, uncovered, over medium heat for 15 minutes, turning to brown evenly. Add tomato mixture. Bring to boiling; reduce heat. Cover and simmer for 35 to 40 minutes, or till chicken is tender and no pink remains. Transfer chicken to a serving platter; keep warm. Skim off fat from tomato mixture. Add chocolate and cook and stir over low heat till chocolate is melted. Pour over chicken. Serve with rice.

Makes 6 servings

Per serving: 435 calories, 29 g protein, 36 g carbohydrate, 20 g total fat (5 g saturated), 69 mg cholesterol, 389 mg sodium, 610 mg potassium

94

STEPS AT A GLANCE	Page
SKINNING CHICKEN	10–11
BRAISING CHICKEN	86

Preparation Time: 20 minutes
Cooking Time: 55 to 60 minutes

INGREDIENTS

2	TO 2-1/2 LB/1 TO 1.25 KG MEATY CHICKEN PIECES (BREASTS, THIGHS, AND DRUMSTICKS), SKIN REMOVED
2	TABLESPOONS COOKING OIL
2	OZ/60 G CHOPPED ONION
2	CLOVES GARLIC, MINCED
10	TO 12 FRESH *OR* TINNED TOMATILLOS, CHOPPED
8	OZ/250 G TINNED TOMATO PURÉE
2	OZ/60 G TOASTED ALMONDS
3/4	OZ/20 G CRUSHED TORTILLA CHIPS
2	FL OZ/60 ML WATER
2	FRESH CHILIES, SEEDED AND CHOPPED, *OR* 2 TINNED WHOLE GREEN CHILIES, SEEDED AND CHOPPED
1/2	OZ/15 G CHOPPED FRESH CORIANDER (CHINESE PARSLEY)
2	TABLESPOONS TOASTED SESAME SEEDS
1/4	TEASPOON GROUND CINNAMON
1/4	TEASPOON SALT
1/8	TEASPOON GROUND CLOVES
1	OZ/30 G SEMISWEET (PLAIN) CHOCOLATE, CUT UP
	HOT COOKED RICE

Fill individual bowls with seasoned rice, then top with braised chicken pieces and mole. Serve flour tortillas for scooping up the gravy, and lime wedges for garnish.

Chicken Filipino-style

Inspired by a classic Filipino recipe, chicken
in coconut sauce is served on a mound of
steamed white rice and garnished with
sliced spring onions.

Preparation Time: 20 minutes
Cooking Time: 35 minutes

INGREDIENTS

2	TO 2-1/2 LB/1 TO 1.25 KG MEATY CHICKEN PIECES (BREASTS, THIGHS, AND DRUMSTICKS)
2	TABLESPOONS COOKING OIL
12	FL OZ/375 ML WATER
3	FL OZ/80 ML CIDER VINEGAR
2	TABLESPOONS SOY SAUCE
3	LARGE CLOVES GARLIC, MINCED
1/2	TEASPOON WHOLE PEPPERCORNS
1/2	TEASPOON GROUND BLACK PEPPER
1	BAY LEAF
1	MEDIUM GREEN PEPPER (CAP-SICUM), SLICED INTO THIN STRIPS
2	TABLESPOONS CORNFLOUR
2	TABLESPOONS WATER
8	FL OZ/250 ML TINNED UNSWEET-ENED COCONUT MILK (NOT CREAM OF COCONUT)
	HOT COOKED RICE
3/4	OZ/20 G SLICED SPRING ONIONS

95

*B*e sure to use unsweetened coconut milk for this
recipe; it is available at most Asian groceries and
at many supermarkets and gourmet shops.

■ If desired, skin chicken. Rinse chicken; pat dry. In a large, heavy frying pan brown chicken
in hot oil, turning to brown evenly. Drain off fat. To the pan add 12 fl oz/375 ml water,
vinegar, soy sauce, garlic, peppercorns, pepper and bay leaf. Bring to boiling; reduce heat.
Cover and simmer for 30 minutes, or till chicken is tender, adding the green pepper strips
during the last 5 minutes of cooking. Transfer chicken to a serving platter; keep warm.

■ With a slotted spoon, remove green pepper strips and set aside. Stir together cornflour and
2 tablespoons water; stir into liquid in frying pan. Cook and stir till thickened and bubbly.
Cook and stir for 2 minutes more. Stir in coconut milk and the green pepper strips. Heat
through, but do not boil. Serve chicken and sauce with rice. Sprinkle with spring onions.
Makes 6 servings

Per serving: 451 calories, 27 g protein, 35 g carbohydrate, 22 g total fat (11 g saturated), 69 mg cholesterol, 414 mg sodium,
415 mg potassium

STEPS AT A GLANCE	Page
BRAISING CHICKEN	86

Chicken Cassoulet

Preparation Time: 20 minutes
Soaking Time: 1 to 24 hours
Cooking Time: 1½ hours
Baking Time: 40 to 45 minutes

INGREDIENTS

10	OZ/300 G DRIED WHITE OR CANNELLINI BEANS
64	FL OZ/2 L WATER
2	OZ/60 G SLICED SPRING ONIONS
1/2	OZ/15 G CHOPPED FRESH PARSLEY
3	FL OZ/80 ML DRY RED OR WHITE WINE
2	SLICES BACON, CRISP-COOKED AND CRUMBLED
1	TABLESPOON TOMATO PASTE
3	CLOVES GARLIC, MINCED
1/2	TEASPOON DRIED THYME, CRUSHED
1	BAY LEAF
6	CHICKEN DRUMSTICKS OR THIGHS (1-1/2 LB/750 G TOTAL)
1	TABLESPOON OLIVE OIL OR COOKING OIL
8	OZ/250 G FULLY COOKED POLISH SAUSAGE OR OTHER PORK SAUSAGE, SLICED INTO 1-IN/ 2.5-CM PIECES

96

*C*assoulet is a French country dish of much renown. If desired, substitute tinned white or cannellini beans, drained and rinsed, for the dried beans. Omit cooking the beans and use water in place of the reserved bean liquid to moisten the cassoulet.

Serve generous portions of just-baked cassoulet with a mixed green salad and crusty bread for a complete meal.

STEPS AT A GLANCE	Page
BRAISING CHICKEN	86

■ Rinse dried beans. In a large saucepan combine beans and 32 fl oz/1 l of the water. Bring to boiling; reduce heat and simmer for 2 minutes. Let stand, covered, for 1 hour. (Or, soak beans in 4 cups water overnight.) Drain beans, discarding water. In the same saucepan combine beans and the remaining 32 fl oz/1 l fresh water. Bring to boiling; reduce heat and simmer for 1½ hours, or till beans are tender. Drain, reserving 5 fl oz/160 ml of the liquid.

■ In a large mixing bowl stir together drained beans, reserved bean liquid, spring onions, parsley, wine, bacon, tomato paste, garlic, thyme, and bay leaf.

■ Rinse chicken; pat dry. In a large, heavy frying pan brown the chicken drumsticks or thighs in hot oil, turning to brown evenly. In a 3-qt/3-l ovenproof casserole layer one third of the beans, all of the chicken, and all of the sausage. Cover with remaining bean mixture. Bake, covered, in a preheated 350°F/180°C oven for 40 to 45 minutes, or till chicken is tender and no pink remains, and beans are heated through.

Makes 6 servings

Per serving: 459 calories, 31 g protein, 35 g carbohydrate, 21 g total fat (6 g saturated), 69 mg cholesterol, 419 mg sodium, 887 mg potassium

Chicken with Greek Olives

STEPS AT A GLANCE	Page
BRAISING CHICKEN	86

Preparation Time: 20 minutes
Cooking Time: 50 to 55 minutes

INGREDIENTS

2	TO 2-1/2 LB/1 TO 1.25 KG MEATY CHICKEN PIECES (BREASTS, THIGHS, AND DRUMSTICKS)
2	TABLESPOONS MARGARINE *OR* BUTTER
4	OZ/125 G FRESH MUSHROOMS, SLICED
2	TABLESPOONS PLAIN FLOUR
1/2	TEASPOON DRIED THYME, CRUSHED
1/4	TEASPOON PEPPER
8	FL OZ/250 ML CHICKEN STOCK
1	TABLESPOON RASPBERRY VINEGAR *OR* RED WINE VINEGAR
2-1/2	OZ/75 G KALAMATA OLIVES, PITTED, *OR* 2-1/2 OZ/75 G SLICED PITTED BLACK OLIVES
	HOT COOKED RICE

*U*se pitted black olives for a mild flavour or brine-soaked Kalamata olives for a more pungent addition to the vinegar-flavoured sauce. Most gourmet food shops stock Mediterranean olives in jars or in bulk.

■ If desired, skin chicken. Rinse chicken; pat dry. In a large, heavy frying pan cook chicken in margarine or butter over medium heat for about 15 minutes, or till chicken is lightly browned, turning occasionally. Reduce heat; cover and simmer for 30 to 35 minutes, or till chicken is tender and no pink remains. Transfer chicken to a serving platter; keep warm.

■ Add mushrooms to frying pan and cook over medium heat for 2 to 3 minutes, or till tender. Stir in flour, thyme, and pepper. Add chicken stock and raspberry vinegar or red wine vinegar all at once. Cook and stir till thickened and bubbly. Cook and stir for 1 minute more. Add olives and heat through. Pour over chicken. Serve with rice.

Makes 4 servings

Per serving: 540 calories, 36 g protein, 35 g carbohydrate, 28 g total fat (6 g saturated), 99 mg cholesterol, 910 mg sodium, 460 mg potassium

Arrange several pieces of this tangy chicken on a plate and spoon on the gravy; serve with rice pilaf and sautéed peppers and eggplant (aubergine).

Balsamic Vinegar Chicken

Another time, serve this easy
dish on pasta instead of rice.

Preparation Time: 20 minutes
Cooking Time: 20 to 22 minutes

INGREDIENTS

2	TABLESPOONS OLIVE OIL *OR* COOKING OIL
4	BONELESS, SKINLESS CHICKEN BREAST HALVES (1 LB/500 G TOTAL)
1/4	TEASPOON WHITE PEPPER
3/4	OZ/20 G CHOPPED SHALLOTS *OR* SPRING ONIONS
8	FL OZ/250 ML CHICKEN STOCK
12	OZ/375 G FRESH ASPARAGUS SPEARS
4	OZ/125 G OYSTER MUSHROOMS *OR* OTHER MUSHROOMS
3	TABLESPOONS BALSAMIC VINEGAR
2	TABLESPOONS MARGARINE *OR* BUTTER, SOFTENED
2	TABLESPOONS TOASTED PINE NUTS
	HOT COOKED RICE

98

*O*yster mushrooms, asparagus, and pine
nuts give crunch and snap to this delicious,
simple braised dish. Oyster mushrooms are an Asian
variety with pale, creamy flesh and a flowerlike cap.

■ In a large, heavy frying pan heat oil over medium-high heat. Add
chicken and cook for 2 minutes. Turn chicken over in pan and sprinkle with white
pepper. Add shallots or spring onions to pan; cook for 2 minutes more. Drain off fat.
Add chicken stock. Bring to boiling; reduce heat. Cover and simmer for 5 minutes.

■ Meanwhile, snap off and discard woody bases from fresh asparagus. Cut asparagus into
2-in/5-cm lengths. Halve any large mushrooms. Add asparagus to frying pan; cover and
cook for 5 to 7 minutes, or till asparagus is just tender and chicken is tender and no pink
remains. Add mushrooms. Cover and cook for 1 minute.

■ Use a slotted spoon to transfer chicken, asparagus, and mushrooms to a serving platter.
Add vinegar to liquid in pan. Bring to boiling; boil over high heat for 5 minutes, or till
liquid is reduced to 3 fl oz/80 ml. Remove pan from heat. Using a wire whisk, blend margarine
or butter into liquid in pan. Spoon over chicken; sprinkle with pine nuts. Serve with rice.

Makes 4 servings

Per serving: 414 calories, 24 g protein, 39 g carbohydrate, 18 g total fat (6 g saturated), 60 mg cholesterol, 301 mg sodium,
642 mg potassium

STEPS AT A GLANCE	Page
SKINNING & BONING CHICKEN	10
BRAISING CHICKEN	86

Braised Chicken with Apple-Cream Sauce

INGREDIENTS

6	BONELESS, SKINLESS CHICKEN BREAST HALVES (1-1/2 LB/750 G TOTAL)
1	TABLESPOON COOKING OIL
2	MEDIUM COOKING APPLES, CORED AND SLICED
1	MEDIUM LEEK, SLICED
4	FL OZ/125 ML APPLE JUICE *OR* APPLE CIDER
1/2	TEASPOON INSTANT CHICKEN STOCK GRANULES *OR* CONCENTRATE
1/4	TEASPOON DRIED THYME, CRUSHED
1/8	TEASPOON WHITE PEPPER
3	FL OZ/80 ML SOUR CREAM
2	TEASPOONS CORNFLOUR

Preparation Time: 25 minutes
Cooking Time: 15 minutes

STEPS AT A GLANCE	Page
SKINNING & BONING CHICKEN	10
BRAISING CHICKEN	86

*S*ince any cut apple surface exposed to air discolours quickly, slice the apples just before cooking them. Rinse the leeks thoroughly before using to remove any dirt that may be hidden between the layers, and slice only the white end.

■ In a large, heavy frying pan brown the chicken breast halves in hot oil over medium heat, turning once. Remove chicken from frying pan. Add the apples and leek to the pan and cook over low heat for 2 minutes. Return the chicken breasts to the pan. Add apple juice or cider and chicken stock granules. Sprinkle with thyme and white pepper. Bring to boiling; reduce heat. Cover and simmer for 10 minutes, or till chicken is tender and no pink remains. Remove chicken from pan; keep warm.

■ In a small mixing bowl stir together sour cream and cornflour. Stir in 2 to 3 tablespoons of the pan juices to thin the mixture; add to remaining pan juices in frying pan. Cook and stir till thickened and bubbly; reduce heat. Cook and stir for 2 minutes more. Spoon sauce over chicken.

Makes 6 servings

Per serving: 219 calories, 22 g protein, 13 g carbohydrate, 8 g total fat (3 g saturated), 65 mg cholesterol, 137 mg sodium, 297 mg potassium

Arrange one chicken breast half on a bed of wild rice and top with sauce, apples, and leek. Serve with vegetables such as marrow in cool weather.

Calypso Curried Chicken

Preparation Time: 15 minutes
Cooking Time: 15 to 20 minutes

INGREDIENTS

8	OZ/250 G TINNED PINEAPPLE PIECES, INCLUDING JUICE
4	BONELESS, SKINLESS CHICKEN BREAST HALVES (1 LB/500 G TOTAL)
1	OZ/30 G PLAIN FLOUR
1	TEASPOON CURRY POWDER
1/2	TEASPOON SALT
1/4	TEASPOON PEPPER
2	TABLESPOONS COOKING OIL
4	OZ/125 G CHOPPED GREEN PEPPER (CAPSICUM)
2-1/2	OZ/75 G CHOPPED ONION
2	CLOVES GARLIC, MINCED
14	OZ/440 G TINNED DICED TOMATOES, INCLUDING JUICE
3	TABLESPOONS DRIED CURRANTS OR RAISINS
1	TEASPOON CURRY POWDER
1/8	TO 1/4 TEASPOON CRUSHED RED (CHILI) PEPPER FLAKES
1/8	TEASPOON SALT
1	TABLESPOON CORNFLOUR
2	TO 3 OZ/60 TO 90 G COARSELY CHOPPED CASHEW PIECES (OPTIONAL)

100

*A*s a result of trade with India during the eigh-
teenth century, this hearty curried chicken dish
became popular in England and the American colonies,
especially in seaports.

For a suitable accompaniment, quickly stir-fry cooked white rice with a little onion, a diced peach, and toasted almonds.

STEPS AT A GLANCE	Page
SKINNING & BONING CHICKEN	10
BRAISING CHICKEN	86

■ Drain pineapple, reserving juice. Set aside. Rinse chicken; pat dry. In a plastic bag combine flour, 1 teaspoon curry powder, ½ teaspoon salt, and pepper. Add chicken breasts, one at a time, and shake to coat well.

■ In a large, heavy frying pan brown the chicken on both sides in hot oil over medium-high heat. Remove chicken from pan. In the oil remaining in the pan, cook green pepper, onion, and garlic till tender but not brown. Stir in drained pineapple, undrained tomatoes, currants, 1 teaspoon curry powder, crushed red pepper flakes, and ⅛ teaspoon salt. Bring mixture to boiling; return chicken to the frying pan. Cover and simmer for 8 to 12 minutes, or till chicken is tender and no pink remains. Remove chicken from the pan; keep warm.

■ Stir together cornflour and reserved pineapple juice; add to tomato mixture. Cook and stir till thickened and bubbly. Cook and stir for 2 minutes more. Serve sauce over chicken. If desired, garnish with cashews.

Makes 4 servings

Per serving: 279 calories, 19 g protein, 30 g carbohydrate, 10 g total fat (2 g saturated), 45 mg cholesterol, 580 mg sodium, 591 mg potassium

Chicken Couscous

Preparation Time: 25 minutes
Cooking Time: 30 minutes

INGREDIENTS

2-1/2	OZ/75 G CHOPPED ONION
1	CLOVE GARLIC, MINCED
1	TABLESPOON OLIVE OIL *OR* COOKING OIL
12	OZ/375 G BONELESS, SKINLESS CHICKEN THIGHS, CUT INTO 1-IN/2.5-CM CUBES
3	MEDIUM CARROTS, CUT INTO 1-IN/2.5-CM PIECES
10	FL OZ/300 ML CHICKEN STOCK
4	OZ/125 G SLICED CELERY
1/2	TEASPOON SALT
1/4	TEASPOON GROUND CUMIN
1/4	TEASPOON GROUND TURMERIC
1/8	TO 1/4 TEASPOON CRUSHED RED (CHILI) PEPPER FLAKES
1	MEDIUM ZUCCHINI (COURGETTE), CUT INTO 1/2 X 1/2 X 1-IN/12-MM X 12-MM X 2.5-CM STRIPS
2	MEDIUM TOMATOES, PEELED, SEEDED, AND CHOPPED
15	OZ/470 G CHICK PEAS (GARBANZO BEANS), TINNED, IN LIQUID, DRAINED
5	OZ/155 G COUSCOUS

*C*ouscous, though it looks like a whole grain, is a tiny, quick-cooking pasta. Served topped with various meats and vegetables, it is a Moroccan staple.

■ In a large, heavy frying pan cook the onion and garlic in hot oil till tender but not brown. Add the chicken, carrots, chicken stock, celery, salt, cumin, turmeric, and crushed red pepper flakes. Bring to boiling; reduce heat. Cover and simmer for 20 minutes. Add the zucchini (courgette), tomatoes, and chick peas. Cover and cook for 10 minutes more, or till chicken and vegetables are tender.

■ Meanwhile, prepare couscous according to package directions. To serve, spoon couscous into a serving bowl. Spoon chicken mixture over couscous.

Makes 4 or 5 servings

Per serving: 502 calories, 27 g protein, 76 g carbohydrate, 10 g total fat (2 g saturated), 41 mg cholesterol, 885 mg sodium, 1,085 mg potassium

STEPS AT A GLANCE	Page
SKINNING & BONING CHICKEN	10
CUTTING CHICKEN CUBES OR STRIPS	72
BRAISING CHICKEN	86

When serving couscous, fluff it up with a fork and top it with chicken, vegetables, and beans for a complete meal. A simple green salad is the only additional accompaniment needed.

Chicken Rouladen

STEPS AT A GLANCE	Page
SKINNING & BONING CHICKEN	10
POUNDING CHICKEN BREASTS	20
BRAISING CHICKEN	86

Preparation Time: 25 minutes
Cooking Time: 30 to 35 minutes

INGREDIENTS

4	BONELESS, SKINLESS CHICKEN BREAST HALVES (1 LB/500 G TOTAL)
4	TEASPOONS HONEY MUSTARD *OR* DIJON-STYLE MUSTARD
4	SLICES THINLY SLICED COOKED HAM (1-1/2 OZ/45 G TOTAL)
8	OZ/250 G ROASTED RED PEPPERS (CAPSICUMS), BOTTLED *OR* TINNED IN JUICE, DRAINED
1	TABLESPOON COOKING OIL
4	FL OZ/125 ML CHICKEN STOCK
4	FL OZ/125 ML DRY WHITE WINE
2	TABLESPOONS TOMATO PASTE
1	TABLESPOON CHOPPED FRESH BASIL *OR* 1/2 TEASPOON DRIED BASIL, CRUSHED
2	TEASPOONS CORNFLOUR
1	TABLESPOON WATER

*I*f you have only enjoyed these rolls prepared with red meat, this version, made with flattened boneless, skinless chicken breasts will be a pleasant, lighter alternative. Cheese-lovers can cover the ham with a thin slice of provolone or Swiss cheese before topping with the roasted red pepper.

■ Rinse chicken; pat dry. Place each breast half between 2 pieces of plastic wrap. Working from the centre to the edges, pound chicken lightly with the flat side of a meat mallet to a ¼-in/6-mm thickness. Remove plastic wrap.

■ Spread each of the chicken breast halves with 1 teaspoon of the mustard. Place a slice of ham on each breast, then a roasted red pepper half. Fold in long sides of chicken and roll up jam-roll style. Secure with wooden toothpicks.

■ In a large, heavy frying pan brown the chicken rolls in hot oil on all sides over medium heat. Add chicken stock and wine. Bring to boiling; reduce heat. Cover and simmer for 25 to 30 minutes, or till chicken is tender and no pink remains. Remove chicken from pan; keep warm.

■ Stir tomato paste and basil into pan. Stir together cornflour and water; stir into pan. Cook and stir till thickened and bubbly. Cook and stir for 1 to 2 minutes more.

Makes 4 servings

Per serving: 207 calories, 24 g protein, 6 g carbohydrate, 7 g total fat (1 g saturated), 62 mg cholesterol, 322 mg sodium, 395 mg potassium

To slice rouladen, remove the cooked chicken rolls to a cutting board and cut across into spirals. Arrange the slices decoratively on a plate and drizzle with pan sauce. Egg noodles and steamed vegetables complete the meal.

102

Chicken Ragoût with Green Olives

INGREDIENTS

3	TABLESPOONS PLAIN FLOUR
1/2	TEASPOON SALT
1/4	TEASPOON PEPPER
12	OZ/375 G BONELESS, SKINLESS CHICKEN THIGHS, CUT INTO 1-IN/2.5-CM CUBES
3	TABLESPOONS COOKING OIL
1	LARGE ONION, CUT INTO WEDGES
2	CLOVES GARLIC, CHOPPED
2	MEDIUM TOMATOES, PEELED, SEEDED, AND CHOPPED, OR 7-1/2 OZ/240 G TINNED TOMATOES, CUT UP, INCLUDING JUICE
1	TABLESPOON TOMATO PASTE
6	FL OZ/180 ML DRY WHITE WINE
6	FL OZ/180 ML CHICKEN STOCK
2	POTATOES, PEELED AND CUT INTO BITE-SIZE PIECES
1	TURNIP, PEELED AND CUT INTO BITE-SIZE PIECES
4	OZ/125 G BABY CARROTS OR 2 MEDIUM CARROTS, CUT INTO 2-IN/5-CM PIECES
1/2	TEASPOON DRIED THYME, CRUSHED
2-1/2	OZ/75 G PIMIENTO-STUFFED GREEN OLIVES, HALVED
1	TABLESPOON CHOPPED FRESH PARSLEY
1	TABLESPOON LEMON JUICE

Spoon the chicken, vegetables, and olives from the pan onto a warm platter and ladle the sauce over the chicken mixture.

*T*he French word for "stew," ragoût, *refers to a cooking method in which the meat is first browned, then cooked slowly in a tasty liquid.*

■ Place flour, salt, and pepper in a plastic bag. Add chicken cubes a few at a time, shaking bag to coat chicken with flour mixture. In a large, heavy frying pan or flameproof casserole dish brown chicken in hot oil, turning to brown evenly. Remove chicken from pan. Set aside.

■ Add onion and garlic to oil remaining in pan and cook for 5 minutes. Add the fresh or undrained tinned tomatoes and tomato paste; cook 5 minutes more, stirring occasionally. Add browned chicken, wine, chicken stock, potatoes, turnip, carrots, and thyme to the pan. Bring to boiling and reduce heat. Cover and simmer for 25 to 30 minutes, or till chicken and vegetables are tender. Add the olives, parsley, and lemon juice; heat through.

Makes 4 servings

Per serving: 378 calories, 18 g protein, 34 g carbohydrate, 17 g total fat (3 g saturated), 41 mg cholesterol, 900 mg sodium, 865 mg potassium

Preparation Time: 15 minutes
Cooking Time: 40 to 45 minutes

STEPS AT A GLANCE	Page
SKINNING & BONING CHICKEN	10
CUTTING CHICKEN CUBES OR STRIPS	72
BRAISING CHICKEN	86

Chicken Goulash

*S*erving a dish made with potatoes spooned over noodles is common in Eastern European cuisine. The flavours and textures mesh beautifully. Spaetzle, tiny German dumplings, are available in most well-stocked supermarkets or delicatessens.

■ In a large, heavy frying pan cook chicken, onion, and garlic in 1 tablespoon hot oil for 3 to 4 minutes, or till chicken is tender and no pink remains. Drain off fat. Add potatoes, tomatoes, 2 fl oz/60 ml water, paprika, salt, caraway seed, marjoram, pepper, and thyme. Bring to boiling; reduce heat. Cover and simmer for 10 to 12 minutes, or till potatoes are tender.

■ Stir together the flour and 2 tablespoons water; stir into chicken mixture. Cook and stir till thickened and bubbly. Cook and stir for 1 minute more. Serve over hot cooked noodles or spaetzle. If desired, serve with sour cream.

Makes 4 servings

Per serving: 219 calories, 15 g protein, 22 g carbohydrate, 8 g total fat (2 g saturated), 41 mg cholesterol, 419 mg sodium, 522 mg potassium

STEPS AT A GLANCE	Page
SKINNING & BONING CHICKEN	10
CUTTING CHICKEN CUBES OR STRIPS	72
BRAISING CHICKEN	86

Preparation Time: 25 minutes
Cooking Time: 17 to 20 minutes

INGREDIENTS

12	OZ/375 G BONELESS, SKINLESS CHICKEN THIGHS, CUT INTO 1-IN/2.5-CM PIECES
4	OZ/125 G CHOPPED ONION
1	CLOVE GARLIC, MINCED
1	TO 2 TABLESPOONS COOKING OIL
2	MEDIUM POTATOES, PEELED AND DICED
7-1/2	OZ/240 G TINNED TOMATOES, CUT UP, INCLUDING JUICE
2	FL OZ/60 ML WATER
1-1/2	TEASPOONS PAPRIKA
1/2	TEASPOON SALT
1/4	TEASPOON CARAWAY SEED
1/4	TEASPOON DRIED MARJORAM, CRUSHED
1/4	TEASPOON PEPPER
	PINCH OF DRIED THYME, CRUSHED
2	TABLESPOONS PLAIN FLOUR
2	TABLESPOONS WATER
	HOT COOKED NOODLES *OR* SPAETZLE
	SOUR CREAM (OPTIONAL)

Divide spaetzle or wide egg noodles among large bowls and cover with goulash. Serve a hearty vegetable as an accompaniment.

Microwaving
& Poaching

Steps in Microwaving Chicken

BASIC TOOLS FOR MICROWAVING CHICKEN

Microwave cooking requires a glass, ceramic, or plastic dish — never metal — waxed paper to prevent spatters during cooking, and tongs to turn the food so that it finishes evenly.

TONGS

11X17-IN/29X43-CM
BAKING DISH

WAXED PAPER

106

NO APPLIANCE DOES a better job than the microwave oven for precooking chicken and for saving you time and cleaning. In 20 minutes or less, poultry pieces are ready to use in salads, soups, casseroles, and more.

Microwave cooking is extremely easy, but it does differ from conventional methods. If you have never used a microwave oven, some background information will be helpful.

Unlike a regular oven, which uses currents of hot, dry air to cook food, a microwave oven bombards a piece of chicken, for example, with short, high-frequency radio waves. These waves cause the moisture inside the food to vibrate and generate heat. One drawback is that food sometimes cooks unevenly unless it is turned or stirred. Another is that cooking can progress in an instant from juicy to overdone, so most recipes suggest that you check for doneness after the minimum cooking time.

Not all baking dishes are microwave safe. Some manufacturers' labels will tell you, but if you are unsure, try the following test: Fill a glass measuring cup with 4 fl oz/ 125 ml water and place the cup and a baking dish without any metal trim in the microwave. Cook on 100 per cent of power output (high) for 1 minute. If the dish stays cool, go ahead and use it. If it gets hot, use something else.

A final caution: Cooking times for microwave recipes are matched to a specific wattage (in this book, 600 to 700 watts). If the wattage of your oven differs, be sure to adjust the timing, or your food will be underdone or overcooked.

BASIC MICROWAVED CHICKEN

Preparation Time: 5 minutes
Cooking Time: 15 to 20 minutes

INGREDIENTS

3   LB/1.5 KG MEATY CHICKEN PIECES (BREASTS, THIGHS, AND DRUM-STICKS)

■ Arrange chicken pieces in a baking dish with meaty portions toward the edges of the dish. Cover with waxed paper. Microwave on 100 per cent of power output (high) for 15 to 20 minutes, or till chicken is tender and no pink remains, rearranging and turning pieces halfway through cooking time. Cool for about 15 minutes. Remove skin and cut or pull meat from the bones. Discard skin and bones and cut up or shred.
Makes about 1½ lb/750 g meat

Per cup: 246 calories, 38 g protein, 0 g carbohydrate, 9 g total fat (2 g saturated), 115 mg cholesterol, 98 mg sodium, 253 mg potassium the chicken pieces can touch, but shouldn't overlap or they won't cook through

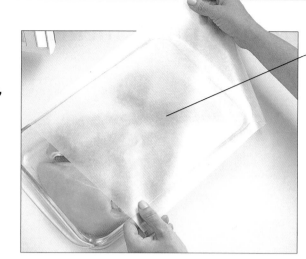

you can also use paper towels or microwave film to cover the food

STEP 1   ARRANGING CHICKEN

Use a microwave-safe dish that is large enough to hold the chicken pieces in a single layer. Arrange the chicken, skin-side up (here the breasts have been skinned), with the meatiest parts toward the edges of the dish.

STEP 2   COVERING CHICKEN WITH WAXED PAPER

Moist chicken will bubble and spatter as it cooks in the microwave. To keep the juices in the baking dish — not on the oven walls — cover the chicken lightly but completely with a sheet of waxed paper; there is no need to seal.

107

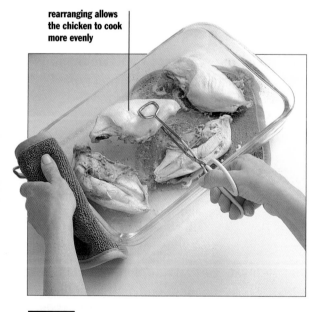

rearranging allows the chicken to cook more evenly

STEP 3   REARRANGING CHICKEN PIECES

Halfway through cooking, pull out the dish with the chicken. With tongs, turn the pieces over and rearrange them so that the less-cooked parts are near the edges of the dish. Cover again with the waxed paper.

Combine tender slices of microwaved chicken breast, seasonal greens, and a favourite vinaigrette for a light meal.

Steps in Poaching Chicken

HEAVY SAUCEPAN
OR COOKING POT

TWO FORKS

BASIC TOOLS FOR POACHING AND SHREDDING CHICKEN

For poaching, use a large enough pot to hold all of the chicken. Transfer the cooked chicken to a cutting board and slice with a sharp knife or shred with a pair of forks.

CUTTING BOARD AND CHEF'S KNIFE

Poaching is a very delicate cooking method that bathes poultry in a gently bubbling liquid just below a boil. The result is moist, succulent meat with a light, clean flavour that is ideal for salads, sandwiches, and soups. Poached poultry, as shown in the recipe on page 114, is also superb on its own with a light sauce. It is low in fat because no oil is needed, but high in flavour because the poaching liquid draws goodness from the meat and bones.

The key to perfectly poached poultry is to keep the heat at a constant temperature throughout cooking. For the most delicious result, select a pot made of a material that will heat evenly and maintain temperature and is large enough to allow the hot liquid to move freely around the chicken pieces.

It is best to let just-cooked poached chicken sit at room temperature for about 15 minutes. This resting period allows the chicken to cool so you can handle it comfortably and also recirculates the juices so they don't pour out when the meat is cut. If desired, return the bones to the pot after removing the meat and simmer for chicken stock (see page 14).

In addition to poaching, the steps opposite demonstrate how to skin, bone, cube, and shred precooked chicken, whether poached, microwaved, or roasted (see Basic Roast Chicken, page 16), to make it ready for the delicious dishes that you'll find in this chapter.

BASIC POACHED CHICKEN

Preparation Time: 5 minutes
Cooking Time: 40 minutes

INGREDIENTS

3   TO 3-1/2 LB/1.5 TO 1.75 KG MEATY CHICKEN PIECES (BREASTS, THIGHS, AND DRUMSTICKS) OR ONE 3- TO 3-1/2-LB/1.5-TO 1.75-KG ROASTING CHICKEN

48 FL OZ/1.5 L WATER

■ Place chicken pieces or whole chicken in a 4½-qt/ 4.5-l heavy saucepan or cooking pot. Add water. Bring to boiling; reduce heat. Cover and simmer for 40 minutes, or till chicken is tender and no pink remains. Remove chicken from liquid. Let cool for about 15 minutes. Remove skin and cut or pull meat from the bones. Discard skin and bones. Cut up or shred as directed.

Makes about 1½ lb/750 g meat

Per cup: 246 calories, 38 g protein, 0 g carbohydrate, 9 g total fat (2 g saturated), 115 mg cholesterol, 98 mg sodium, 253 mg potassium

for poaching,
bubbles should
barely break
the surface of
the liquid

STEP 1 POACHING CHICKEN

Place meaty chicken pieces or a whole chicken in a
large cooking pot. Add water to cover (about 48 fl oz/
1.5 l) and bring to a boil. Reduce heat to low, cover
with the lid, and simmer until tender.

STEP 2 REMOVING THE SKIN AND MEAT

Set the cooled poached chicken on a cutting board.
Pull off the skin and discard. The meat should be
tender enough that it will release from the bone with
a light tug. If not, cut away with a knife.

109

use cooked chicken
right away or store,
well wrapped, in the
refrigerator for a short
time until needed

STEP 3 CUTTING UP COOKED CHICKEN

Once the skin is removed and the meat taken off the
bone, the cooked chicken can be cut up to suit any
recipe. Use a sharp knife and cut it into slices,
or cut it into cubes by cutting the slices crosswise.

pull with the
grain of the
meat to shred it

STEP 4 SHREDDING COOKED CHICKEN

Some recipes for soups and salads require shredded
chicken meat. To shred, steady a piece of cooked boned,
skinned chicken with a fork and pull the fibres apart
with a second fork.

Parmesan Gougère with Chicken Filling

INGREDIENTS

GOUGÈRE

8	FL OZ/250 ML WATER
4	OZ/125 G BUTTER OR MARGARINE
1/8	TEASPOON SALT
4	OZ/125 G PLAIN FLOUR
4	EGGS
2	OZ/60 G FINELY GRATED FRESH PARMESAN CHEESE
2	TABLESPOONS FINELY GRATED FRESH PARMESAN CHEESE

FILLING

2	TABLESPOONS MARGARINE OR BUTTER
4	OZ/125 G SLICED CARROTS
3	OZ/90 G FRESH MUSHROOMS, QUARTERED
4	OZ/125 G SLICED ZUCCHINI (COURGETTES)
2-1/2	OZ/75 G CHOPPED ONION
6	FL OZ/180 ML CHICKEN STOCK
2	TABLESPOONS PLAIN FLOUR
1	TEASPOON DRIED ITALIAN SEASONING, CRUSHED
1/4	TEASPOON SALT
1/4	TEASPOON PEPPER
12	OZ/375 G CHOPPED COOKED CHICKEN
2	OZ/60 G SHREDDED PROVOLONE OR MOZZARELLA CHEESE
1	MEDIUM TOMATO, PEELED, SEEDED, AND CHOPPED

*T*raditionally, the savoury baked choux pastry known as gougère is made with Gruyère cheese; here we've used Parmesan and shaped the pastry as a shell for filling.

■ For gougère, in a medium saucepan combine water, butter or margarine, and salt. Bring to boiling. Add flour all at once, stirring vigorously. Cook and stir till the mixture forms a ball that does not separate. Remove from heat. Cool for 10 minutes. Add eggs, one at a time, beating with a wooden spoon after each addition till smooth. Stir in the 2 oz/60 g Parmesan cheese. Spread mixture over the bottom and up the sides of a well-greased 10-in/25-cm pie plate with high sides. Sprinkle with the remaining Parmesan cheese. Bake in a preheated 400°F/200°C oven for 30 to 40 minutes, or till golden brown.

■ Meanwhile, for filling, in a large frying pan melt margarine or butter over medium heat. Add the carrots, mushrooms, zucchini (courgettes), and onion. Cook and stir for about 5 minutes, or till vegetables are just tender.

■ Stir together chicken stock, flour, Italian seasoning, salt, and pepper. Cook and stir till thickened and bubbly. Cook and stir for 1 minute more. Stir in the cooked chicken, Provolone or mozzarella cheese, and tomato. Heat through. Fill hot gougère shell with the hot filling. Serve immediately.

Makes 6 servings

Per serving: 402 calories, 14 g protein, 24 g carbohydrate, 28 g total fat (15 g saturated), 196 mg cholesterol, 763 mg sodium, 336 mg potassium

Preparation Time: 15 minutes
Baking Time: 30 to 40 minutes
Cooking Time: 10 minutes

STEPS AT A GLANCE	Page
MAKING GOUGÈRE DOUGH	110
MICROWAVING OR POACHING	106–109

110

STEPS IN MAKING GOUGÈRE DOUGH

STEP 1 STIRRING DOUGH

In a medium saucepan, combine water, butter, and salt; bring to a boil. Add flour and stir vigorously until dough pulls away from sides of the pan.

STEP 2 FINAL STIRRING

Let the mixture cool before adding the eggs. After the last egg has been added, the dough will lose its lumpiness and be smooth and satiny.

STEP 3 SHAPING GOUGÈRE

Blend in cheese and spread dough over the bottom and up the sides of a well-greased pie plate.

Essentially a one-dish meal, this filled
gougère needs only a salad accompaniment and an inviting dessert such as
fresh fruit and sweet biscuits.

Before preparing these salads, let the chicken chill thoroughly. Then arrange lettuce leaves on individual plates to serve as a base and top with a portion of the chicken mixture.

Chicken & Potato Salad with Olive Mayonnaise

Preparation Time: 25 minutes
Cooking Time: 10 to 15 minutes
Chilling Time: 2 hours

INGREDIENTS

OLIVE MAYONNAISE

4	OZ/125 G PITTED GREEN OLIVES, DRAINED
2	FL OZ/60 ML REFRIGERATED OR THAWED FROZEN EGG PRODUCT, OR 1 EGG
2	TABLESPOONS LEMON JUICE
1	CLOVE GARLIC, PEELED
1/2	TEASPOON DRY MUSTARD
1/4	TEASPOON SALT
1/8	TEASPOON GROUND RED (CAYENNE) PEPPER
8	FL OZ/250 ML OLIVE OIL

SALAD

1	LB/500 G TINY NEW POTATOES
12	OZ/375 G COOKED CHICKEN CUT INTO 3/4-IN/2-CM CUBES
1-1/2	OZ/45 G FINELY CHOPPED RED PEPPER (CAPSICUM)
3/4	OZ/20 G FINELY CHOPPED SPRING ONION
	LETTUCE LEAVES

*I**f you prefer a milder flavour, use ripe black olives instead of green olives. The mayonnaise can be made with pasturized liquid egg product, which contains less cholesterol, or with a whole egg.*

■ For olive mayonnaise, in a food processor bowl or blender container combine olives, egg product or egg, lemon juice, garlic, mustard, salt, and ground red pepper. Process or blend till olives are puréed. With the processor or blender running, add oil in a thin, steady stream. (When necessary, stop the machine and use a rubber spatula to clean the sides of the bowl.) Set aside 8 fl oz/250 ml. Cover and store remaining mayonnaise in the refrigerator for up to 2 weeks.

■ For salad, cut potatoes into quarters. In a medium saucepan cook potatoes, covered, in a small amount of boiling lightly salted water for 10 to 15 minutes or till tender; drain. In a large mixing bowl stir together potatoes, the 8 fl oz/250 ml olive mayonnaise, the cooked chicken, red pepper, and spring onion. Cover and chill for at least 2 hours. Serve on lettuce leaves.

Makes 4 servings

Per serving: 610 calories, 26 g protein, 28 g carbohydrate, 45 g total fat (7 g saturated), 68 mg cholesterol, 571 mg sodium, 805 mg potassium

STEPS AT A GLANCE	Page
MAKING OLIVE MAYONNAISE	**113**
MICROWAVING OR POACHING	**106–109**

113

STEPS IN MAKING OLIVE MAYONNAISE

STEP 1 PURÉEING OLIVES

Combine pitted green olives, egg product or egg, lemon juice, and seasonings in the work bowl of a food processor or blender. Process until the olives are chopped to a purée; scrape down the sides of the bowl with a rubber spatula.

STEP 2 ADDING OIL

With the machine running, pour olive oil into the work bowl in a thin, continuous stream. If necessary, stop the motor and clean the sides of the bowl once again so that all of the purée is incorporated.

Poached Chicken with Star Anise & Ginger

*C*ut the ginger root into pieces that are large enough to be noticed; the ginger imparts *a wonderful flavour that should stand out. While star anise, an ancient Oriental spice, is not a true anise, it adds an intriguing hint of licorice to the sauce.*

■ Rinse chicken; pat dry. In a heavy saucepan or cooking pot combine water, soy sauce, brown sugar, ginger liqueur or wine, ginger root, and star anise. Place the chicken, breast-side down, in the pot. Bring to boiling; reduce heat. Cover and simmer for 25 minutes. Turn chicken over and simmer, covered, for 25 to 30 minutes more, or till chicken is tender and no pink remains, basting frequently during the last 10 minutes. Remove chicken from pan; keep warm.

■ Skim fat from cooking liquid. Strain liquid through several layers of pure cotton cheese-cloth; discard ginger and anise. Reserve 12 fl oz/375 ml of the liquid; discard remaining liquid. Return the reserved liquid to the pot. Boil, uncovered, for 3 to 4 minutes, or till reduced to 4 fl oz/125 ml.

■ To serve, cut the chicken into serving-sized pieces. Spoon some of the reduced liquid over each serving and hand around the remainder. Garnish with spring onion strips.

Makes 6 servings

Per serving: 277 calories, 26 g protein, 14 g carbohydrate, 12 g total fat (3 g saturated), 79 mg cholesterol, 691 mg sodium, 269 mg potassium

114

Juicy poached chicken topped with a subtle sauce is delicious with noodles and stir-fried Asian-style vegetables.

STEPS AT A GLANCE	Page
POACHING CHICKEN	108

Preparation Time: 15 minutes
Cooking Time: 55 to 60 minutes

INGREDIENTS

1	3- TO 3-1/2-LB/1.5- TO 1.75-KG WHOLE ROASTING CHICKEN
16	FL OZ/500 ML WATER
6	FL OZ/180 ML SOY SAUCE
3-1/2	OZ/105 G BROWN SUGAR
3	TABLESPOONS GINGER LIQUEUR *OR* DRY WHITE WINE
1	TABLESPOON THINLY SLICED FRESH GINGER ROOT
2	WHOLE STAR ANISE
2	SPRING ONIONS, CUT INTO THIN STRIPS

Island Chicken Sandwiches

STEPS AT A GLANCE	Page
POACHING CHICKEN	108

Preparation Time: 25 minutes
Cooking Time: 40 minutes

INGREDIENTS

1	3- TO 3-1/2-LB/1.5- TO 1.75-KG ROASTING CHICKEN, CUT UP
48	FL OZ/1.5 L WATER
1	TEASPOON FINELY SHREDDED LIME PEEL
2	FL OZ/60 ML FRESH LIME JUICE
1/2	TEASPOON SALT
1/4	TEASPOON LEMON PEPPER
3/4	OZ/20 G FLAKED COCONUT
1-1/2	OZ/45 G FINELY CHOPPED SPRING ONION
2	SMALL HOT CHILIES, FINELY CHOPPED
	PITA BREAD ROUNDS OR FLOUR TORTILLAS OR BREAD ROLLS
	SPINACH LEAVES AND/OR PEELED AND SLICED PAWPAW OR MANGO

115

F or best flavour, use freshly grated lime peel and fresh lime juice. You will be able to extract more juice if the lime is at room temperature and you roll it back and forth under your palm a few times before squeezing it. Be sure to wear gloves when handling fresh chilies to protect your eyes and skin against burning.

■ Rinse chicken; pat dry. Place chicken in a 4½-qt/4.5-l heavy saucepan or cooking pot. Add water. Bring to boiling; reduce heat. Simmer, covered, for 40 minutes, or till chicken is tender and no pink remains. Remove chicken from pot; reserve the stock for another use. When cool enough to handle, skin, bone, and shred chicken.

■ In a large mixing bowl combine warm chicken, lime peel, lime juice, salt, and lemon pepper; toss to mix. Stir in coconut, spring onion, and chilies.

■ Line pita pockets, hollowed-out rolls or tortillas with spinach and/or pawpaw or mango and add chicken mixture; roll up the flour tortillas, if using.

Makes 4 to 6 servings

Per serving: 246 calories, 38 g protein, 0 g carbohydrate, 9 g total fat (3 g saturated), 84 mg cholesterol, 784 mg sodium, 692 mg potassium

Stuff this tropical chicken salad into pita bread or a hollowed-out bread roll, or roll in a tortilla, for a light lunch to eat with your fingers.

Taipei Chicken with Mixed Greens

STEPS AT A GLANCE	Page
MICROWAVING OR POACHING	106–109

Preparation Time: 20 minutes
Cooking Time: 3 to 5 minutes

INGREDIENTS

12	OZ/375 G SHREDDED COOKED CHICKEN, WARMED
3	OZ/90 G PACKAGED CRISP CHOW MEIN NOODLES
3/4	OZ/20 G THINLY SLICED SPRING ONIONS
2	FL OZ/60 ML SOY SAUCE
2	TABLESPOONS SESAME OIL
2	TABLESPOONS RICE VINEGAR
2	TABLESPOONS WATER
2	TEASPOONS SUGAR
2	TEASPOONS GRATED FRESH GINGER ROOT
1	SMALL HOT RED *OR* GREEN CHILI, SEEDED AND FINELY CHOPPED (1 TABLESPOON)
12	OZ/375 G MIXED FRESH SALAD GREENS

For a light meal, toss warm shredded chicken with a hot soy-sesame sauce. Arrange fresh greens on individual plates and cover with a portion of the chicken.

*Y*ou could add about 4 fl oz/125 ml wine or dry sherry to the poach-ing liquid or to the microwave dish when cooking the chicken to add flavour and help keep the meat moist.

■ In a large mixing bowl combine the chicken, chow mein noodles, and spring onions.
■ In a small saucepan stir together soy sauce, sesame oil, vinegar, water, sugar, ginger root, and chili. Bring to boiling, stirring to dissolve the sugar. Remove from heat and pour over the chicken mixture. Toss to mix. Serve on mixed salad greens.
Makes 4 servings

Per serving: 316 calories, 26 g protein, 15 g carbohydrate, 17 g total fat (3 g saturated), 68 mg choles-terol, 1,117 mg sodium, 529 mg potassium

Curried Chicken Salad

*T*ry other fruits in this salad, such as apples, red or
green seedless grapes, or pineapple. Two tablespoons
of golden raisins or dried currants may also be added.

- Chop any large pieces of fruit in the chutney. In a small
mixing bowl stir together chutney, mayonnaise or salad
dressing, and curry powder.
- Coarsely chop 2 oz/60 g of the almonds. In a large mixing
bowl combine chicken, pears, and chopped almonds. Add
mayonnaise mixture and mix well. Cover and chill for 2
to 24 hours. Serve on spinach-lined plates. Garnish with
remaining whole almonds.

Makes 4 to 6 servings

Per serving: 532 calories, 28 g protein, 24 g carbohydrate, 38 g total fat
(6 g saturated), 84 mg cholesterol, 406 mg sodium, 744 mg potassium

Preparation Time: 15 minutes
Chilling Time: 2 to 24 hours

INGREDIENTS

2	TABLESPOONS CHUTNEY
4	FL OZ/125 ML MAYONNAISE *OR* SALAD DRESSING
1/2	TEASPOON CURRY POWDER
3	OZ/90 G LIGHTLY SALTED WHOLE ALMONDS
12	OZ/375 G CHOPPED COOKED CHICKEN
2	BROWN *OR* RIPE GREEN UNPEELED PEARS, CORED AND COARSELY CHOPPED
	SPINACH LEAVES

STEPS AT A GLANCE	Page
MICROWAVING OR POACHING	106–109

117

Add a touch of heat to this cool
salad by adding spicy chutney
to the dressing.

GLOSSARY

The following glossary provides information on selecting, purchasing, and storing ingredients used in this book. Groups of ingredients are arranged clockwise from the upper left and are described in the text accordingly.

BASIL

BAY LEAF

CHILIES

COCONUT MILK

EGGPLANT (AUBERGINE)

FENNEL

HOT BEAN PASTE

LEEKS

MUSHROOMS

OLIVES

BASIL An intensely aromatic green-leafed herb, basil has a sweet-to-peppery licorice flavour that enhances tomato-based dishes and sauces, and Italian pesto. Fresh basil is plentiful in summer; dried basil is always available in supermarket spice sections. Immerse freshly cut stems in 2 in/5 cm of water, cover with a plastic bag, and refrigerate for several days.

BAY LEAF Pungent, woody bay leaves, from the evergreen bay tree, add a distinctive flavour to soups, stews, and marinades. Add whole leaves during cooking, then remove before serving. Dried bay leaves are on all supermarket spice shelves; store airtight in a cool, dark spot and use within a year.

CHILIES These range from mildly hot to roof-raising and can be red, yellow or green; they are sold fresh or tinned and pickled. Finely ground red pepper (ground chilies, cayenne), and red pepper flakes, all hot and pungent blends of dried red chilies, are sold as spices. Hot peppers contain oils that burn eyes and skin, so always wear rubber gloves or protect your hands with plastic bags when cutting up any fresh chili.

COCONUT MILK A staple ingredient in Thai curries and used in beverages, sauces, soups, and desserts throughout Southeast Asia, unsweetened coconut milk is made from water and coconut pulp. Rich and creamy, it is available in tins at supermarkets or Asian groceries. Do not substitute cream of coconut.

EGGPLANT (AUBERGINE) This versatile vegetable is available in several forms, most commonly the large, pear-shaped Western or Italian type and the slender Asian varieties. Most are purple-skinned, although some are white. When cooked, all eggplants have a mild flavour and tender, creamy flesh. Look for plump, glossy, heavy eggplants with taut skin and no bruises or scratches. Refrigerate in a plastic bag for up to 2 days.

FENNEL A creamy-white to pale-green vegetable with a broad, bulbous base, tubular stalks, and feathery leaves, fennel has a texture like celery and faint licorice flavour that becomes more delicate when cooked. Select bulbs that are free of cracks or brown spots. Refrigerate in a plastic bag for up to 4 days.

HOT BEAN PASTE Made from a fermented soybean sauce and crushed hot chilies, this Asian cooking condiment thickens and sharpens the flavours of all kinds of foods. Look for it in jars or tins in the Asian food section of well-stocked supermarkets. Stays fresh indefinitely in the refrigerator.

LEEKS This distinctive member of the onion family resembles a giant spring onion, but is much more mildly flavoured. Small-to-medium, healthy-looking leeks with crisp green leaves are the best choice; large ones (over 1½ in/4 cm in diameter) tend to be tough. Refrigerate in a plastic bag for up to 5 days. Before using, rinse leeks carefully, as dirt tends to get trapped between the layers.

MUSHROOMS A fungus, mushrooms appear in the market in numerous varieties, colours, and sizes. Common or button mushrooms are white, cream, and brown, with a mild flavour and a characteristic dome on a stubby stem. Shiitakes are an Asian variety with floppy, meaty dark-brown caps and tough, thin stems that are usually trimmed off and discarded. Select firm, fresh, plump mushrooms that aren't slimy or bruised. Store in the refrigerator, lightly wrapped in paper towels or in a paper bag, never in plastic. Use immediately.

OLIVES The fruit of the silvery-leafed olive tree, olives are either cured for eating or pressed for their oil. There are dozens of varieties, both green and black. The former are under-ripe, with a salty, tart flavour; they are packed

PAPRIKA

PARSLEY

SAFFRON

SAGE

SESAME OIL

pitted or unpitted in jars or tins. Pitted green olives are sometimes stuffed with red pimiento, tiny onions, or whole blanched almonds. Black olives, including Kalamatas, are ripe, with a smooth, mellow flavour. Buy them in tins, jars, or loose.

PAPRIKA Ground from dried, mild chilies, paprika adds a dash of red to dressings, stews, egg and rice dishes, and sausages. Imported sweet or hot Hungarian paprika is more pungent than the mild Spanish type. Most supermarkets stock paprika in their spice section. Store in a cool, dry spot.

PARSLEY This widely used, bright-green herb adds a clean, fresh flavour and decorative colour to almost any dish. Curly-leaf parsley is ruffled, with a slightly peppery taste; Italian parsley is flat-leafed and more pungent. The leaves of the coriander plant are also known as Chinese parsley, or cilantro. Select healthy-looking bunches that aren't wilted or brown. To store, rinse and shake off excess moisture. Wrap in paper towels, then in a plastic bag, and refrigerate for up to 1 week.

SAFFRON At least 225,000 stigmas from a special variety of crocus are needed to make just 1 lb/500 g of yellow-orange saffron, the world's costliest spice. Luckily, most dishes only require a small amount. For the most flavour, saffron threads or powder should be steeped in hot liquid. The threads stay pungent longer than the powder; both are available where spices are sold.

SAGE Grey-green sage is a fragrant herb with a slightly bitter flavour and distinctive aroma. It is widely used with poultry and is a staple seasoning for sausage. Wash the leaves and shake off excess water; wrap in paper towels and refrigerate in a plastic bag for up to 1 week. Dried sage is stocked with other seasonings in all supermarkets. Bottled dry leaves will keep for up to 2 years and ground sage for up to 6 months.

SESAME OIL This smells like the sesame seed it was pressed from. In Asia, it is not used for cooking, but rather as a seasoning for its nutty flavour. Most well-stocked supermarkets carry it, as do Asian groceries.

SHALLOTS This diminutive member of the onion family is formed in the same way as garlic, with a head made up of more than one clove. Shallots have a milder flavour than most onions and need only quick cooking. Look for firm, well-shaped heads that are not sprouting. Store in a cool, dry place for up to 1 month.

SWEET PEPPERS (CAPSICUMS) Sweet peppers, or capsicums, are mildly flavoured, with a crisp, crunchy texture. Green ones are most common, but orange, red and yellow are available at greengrocers and supermarkets. Choose firm, shiny, unbruised peppers. Store for up to 5 days in the refrigerator.

THYME Spicy and pungent, thyme is rarely used alone. More often, it is blended with other herbs to give complexity to poultry, veal, and other dishes. It is sold fresh and dried. Store fresh thyme wrapped in paper towels in a plastic bag; refrigerate for 1 week. Store dried thyme for up to 2 years.

TOMATILLOS Despite their similar name, tomatillos are not tomatoes but rather small, green ground cherries with a papery brown husk. Their tart, lemony flavour adds a bite to Mexican sauces and stews. They are available fresh at gourmet greengrocers, and tinned at well-stocked supermarkets. Choose fresh, firm tomatillos with tight-fitting husks; refrigerate in a paper bag for up to 10 days.

VINEGAR Expose alcohol to a particular strain of airborne bacteria and it becomes vinegar. This acidic liquid enlivens salad dressings, marinades, and sauces, as well as vegetables and noodles. Italian balsamic vinegar is aged in wooden barrels for several years to darken and mellow. Cider vinegar is a pale, golden brown with a fruity, faintly apple flavour. Wine vinegar, both red and white, gets its character from the particular wine used to make it. Vinegar lasts indefinitely, but it is best to store it away from light and heat.

SHALLOTS

SWEET PEPPERS (CAPSICUMS)

THYME

TOMATILLOS

VINEGAR

INDEX

Recipes

Alsatian-style chicken and dumplings 90–91
Balsamic vinegar chicken 98
Basic microwaved chicken 106
Basic poached chicken 108
Basic roast chicken 16
Braised chicken with apple-cream sauce 99
Butterflied citrus chicken 42–43
Calypso curried chicken 100
Carolina-style oven-barbecued chicken 32
Chicken and potato salad with olive mayonnaise 112–113
Chicken breasts
　balsamic vinegar chicken 98
　braised chicken with apple-cream sauce 99
　calypso curried chicken 100
　chicken Cantonese 74–75
　chicken Diana 65
　chicken fajitas 63
　chicken piccata with vegetables 66
　chicken provençale 56–57
　chicken rouladen 102
　chicken salad niçoise 46
　chicken with artichokes 84
　chicken with duxelles wrapped in phyllo 67
　crystal chicken with broccoli 76–77
　ginger chicken with peas and shiitakes 83
　Japanese chicken kebabs 44
　sautéed breasts with beurre blanc 54–55
　sautéed chicken sandwich with olives 69
　sherried chicken with orange sauce 64
　stuffed, with red pepper coulis 34
　sweet and sour chicken 80
　with sauce suprême 68
　with tomato-mint pesto 40–41
Chicken stock 14
Chicken Cantonese 74–75
Chicken cassoulet 96
Chicken couscous 101
Chicken Diana 65
Chicken fajitas 63
Chicken Filipino-style 95
Chicken goulash 104
Chicken legs
　Carolina-style oven-barbecued chicken 32

chicken with spicy yogurt sauce 92–93
coconut chicken 61
honey-glazed drumsticks 45
with beer barbecue sauce 62
Chicken mole 94
Chicken piccata with vegetables 66
Chicken pieces
　Alsatian-style chicken and dumplings 90–91
　chicken and potato salad with olive mayonnaise 112–113
　chicken Filipino-style 95
　chicken mole 94
　chicken stock 14
　chicken with Greek olives 97
　crispy fried chicken 58
　curried chicken salad 117
　hearty coq au vin 88–89
　Island chicken sandwiches 115
　Parmesan gougère with chicken filling 110–111
　Taipei chicken with mixed greens 116
　tangy marinated fried chicken 59
Chicken provençale 56–57
Chicken ragout with green olives 103
Chicken rouladen 102
Chicken salad niçoise 46
Chicken thighs
　chicken cassoulet 96
　chicken couscous 101
　chicken goulash 104
　chicken ragout with green olives 103
　chicken with artichokes 84
　firecracker chicken thighs 48
　pepper stir-fry 82
　sautéed chicken with fresh tomato chutney 60
　sesame chicken with vegetables 79
　spicy Spanish kebabs 47
　stir-fried chicken thighs with fresh asparagus 81
　Thai-style chicken and spinach 78
Chicken wings, smoky 33

Chicken with artichokes 84
Chicken with duxelles wrapped in phyllo 67
Chicken with Greek olives 97
Chicken with lemon stuffing 24–25
Chicken with roasted garlic sauce 29
Chicken with spicy yogurt sauce 92–93
Coconut chicken 61
Crispy fried chicken 58
Crystal chicken with broccoli 76–77
Curried chicken salad 117
Fajitas, chicken 63
Firecracker chicken thighs 48
Ginger chicken with peas and shiitakes 83
Ground chicken
　Rhineland chicken burgers 70
Hearty coq au vin 88–89
Honey-glazed drumsticks 45
Island chicken sandwiches 115
Japanese chicken kebabs 44
Parmesan gougère with chicken filling 110–111
Pepper stir-fry 82
Poached chicken with star anise and ginger 114
Poussins roasted with vegetable stuffing 30
Poussins with cherry sauce 31
Rhineland chicken burgers 70
Roast chicken with chili-coriander butter 26–27
Roast chicken with minted spice rub 28
Roast chicken with pecan rice stuffing 22–23
Sautéed breasts with beurre blanc 54–55
Sautéed chicken sandwich with olives 69
Sautéed chicken with fresh tomato chutney 60
Sesame chicken with vegetables 79
Sherried chicken with orange sauce 64
Smoky chicken wings 33

Spicy Spanish kebabs 47
Stir-fried chicken thighs with fresh asparagus 81
Stock, chicken 14
Stuffed chicken breasts with red pepper coulis 34
Sweet and sour chicken 80
Taipei chicken with mixed greens 116
Tangy marinated fried chicken 59
Thai-style chicken and spinach 78
Whole chicken
　basic roast chicken 16
　butterflied citrus chicken 42–43
　chicken with lemon stuffing 24–25
　chicken with roasted garlic sauce 29
　poached chicken with star anise and ginger 114
　roast chicken with chili-coriander butter 26–27
　roast chicken with minted spice rub 28
　roast chicken with pecan rice stuffing 22–23

Steps

Beurre blanc, making 54
Broccoli, trimming 77
Chicken
　baking boneless breasts 20–21
　barbecuing 38–39
　braising 86–87
　butterflying whole 43
　carving 18–19
　cutting up whole 8–9
　deep-frying 77
　grilling 36–37
　microwaving 106–107
　pan-frying 50–51
　poaching 108–109
　roasting 16–17
　sautéing 52–53
　scoring and marinating 92
　seasoning, under the skin 27
　skinning and boning 10–11
　stir-frying 72–73
　stock, making 14
　storing 12–13
　stuffing 22
Croutons, making 89
Dumplings, making 90
Gougère dough, making 110
Gravy, making 24
Herbs, preparing 57
Olive mayonnaise, making 113
Pockets, making 40
Stir-fry ingredients, preparing 74
Tomatoes, preparing 57

120

USING THE NUTRITION ANALYSIS

Keep track of your daily nutrition needs by using the information we provide at the end of each recipe. We've analysed the nutritional content of each recipe serving for you. When a recipe gives an ingredient substitution, we used the first choice in the analysis. If it makes a range of servings (such as 4 to 6), we used the smaller number. Ingredients listed as optional weren't included in the calculations. To convert calories to kilojoules, multiply by a factor of 4.2.